TRÍONA DOHERTY *and* JANE MELLETT

DELVE DEEPER

Exploring the Sunday Gospels
in the Year of Luke

**TWENTY-THIRD
PUBLICATIONS**
twentythirdpublications.com

Twenty-Third Publications
One Montauk Avenue, Suite 200
New London, CT 06320
(860) 437-3012 or (800) 321-0411
www.twentythirdpublications.com

This edition is published by arrangement
with Messenger Publications, Dublin, Ireland.

Cover image: ©Shutterstock.com / Erik Ao

ISBN: 978-1-62785-653-9
Printed in the U.S.A.

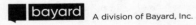 A division of Bayard, Inc.

CONTENTS

ACKNOWLEDGMENTS

This book would not have come into being without the initial invitation from Francis Cousins to write "The Deep End" column for *Intercom* magazine. We would like to thank him for sowing the seed and the subsequent editors of *Intercom* for their ongoing support.

It has been a pleasure to work with the team at Messenger Publications, in particular, Donal Neary, SJ, Patrick Carberry, SJ, Carolanne Henry, Kate Kiernan, Paula Nolan, and Cecilia West. We would like to most sincerely thank Fr. Donal, who from the outset was extremely welcoming to us and open to this project.

We are grateful to Dr. Dermot Lane for his support from the early days of this project and for his positive and encouraging words in the Foreword. Sincere thanks also to Dr. Jessie Rogers, Dean of the Faculty of Theology, St. Patrick's College, Maynooth, for her warm endorsement.

Thank you to Fr. Paddy Jones, former director of the National Centre for Liturgy, who was extremely helpful in answering our queries on the liturgical calendar.

A heartfelt thank you to our friends Sarah Adams, Christy Hicks, Nóirín Lynch, and Sylvia Thompson, all of whom read early drafts and offered insightful and helpful comments.

A special debt of gratitude goes to Fr. Brendan McConvery CSsR, Emeritus Lecturer in Sacred Scripture, and Dr. Séamus O'Connell, Professor of Sacred Scripture, St. Patrick's College, Maynooth. Ever since our first year studying theology in

Maynooth, and through our postgraduate studies, they have inspired our love of Scripture and continue to break open the word for many people across this island.

Finally, thank you to our families, in particular Mary and Cahir Doherty, Pat and Samuel Doyle, and Margaret, Gerry and Gerard Mellett, for their constant support, and to all who encouraged us to take the plunge and make this book a reality.

FOREWORD

It is a pleasure to offer a Foreword to *Delve Deeper: Exploring the Sunday Gospels in the Year of Luke* and to warmly welcome its publication. I read this book from beginning to end and came away feeling I had been on a weekend retreat: spiritually renewed, biblically nourished, and theologically energized.

Delve Deeper offers an inspiring commentary on the gospel reading of every Sunday of the year of St. Luke. In addition, it presents helpful introductions to *Lectio Divina*, the liturgical seasons of the year, feast days, and Ordinary Time. The approach taken is one of analyzing the gospel text, followed by an application of its message to a contemporary life situation, and an invitation to "Go Deeper." This approach offers the reader an opportunity to get inside the living word of God each Sunday and apply it in a practical way to life and living.

The range of references throughout the book gives an indication of the spiritual breadth and depth of these homilies: among them are Thomas Merton, J.R.R. Tolkien, Marilynne Robinson, Mahatma Gandhi, Margaret Silf, James Martin, Richard Rohr, Ronald Rolheiser, Joan Chittister, Mary T. Malone, Arundhati Roy, and Rebecca Solnit.

I can hear some asking the question, "Do we really need another book of homilies?" My answer is, yes, we do need *these* particular gospel reflections. Here we have the voices of two women engaging constructively with the gospel readings for each Sunday. These particular voices see things in the text that men have often missed, such as the significant role of Mary, the place of women disciples in the ministry of Jesus, the witness of the women at the cross of Calvary, and the proclamation by women of the good news of the resurrection. The book is also unique in the way it engages the ecological crisis and emphasizes the importance of the Season of Creation as a lens for understanding the gospel readings.

This book is full of spiritual insights, containing nuggets of wisdom and a deep awareness of the climate challenges facing humanity, as outlined in Pope Francis's encyclical on care for our common home, *Laudato Si'*. Further, alongside the important attention given to women and creation in the gospels, there is a deep, biblically based spirituality informing these pages. The spirituality in question is not "soft"; rather, it has a prophetic edge to it, making demands on the reader and challenging all to live out the values of the Reign of God in this life.

The authors of this new book, Jane Mellet and Tríona Doherty, have impressive credentials. Specializing in Bible studies, both have MAs in theology from St. Patrick's College, Maynooth, and both have wide experience of working in a variety of ministries in the Church.

I recommend this book enthusiastically to bishops, priests, ministers of the word, liturgy groups, chaplains, catechists, and religious educators. The book could also be used by those who would like to start *Lectio Divina* in their parish or establish a Bible study group or conduct a book club on the Sunday gospels. I commend it enthusiastically to all who are charged with the responsibility of breaking open the living word of God as "food for the soul" on the journey of Christian life. It is a great resource and a valuable companion for those who want to go deeper into the gospel readings.

Easter 2021
DR. DERMOT A. LANE,
Balally Parish, Dublin 16.

Welcome

"Put out into the deep" (LUKE 5:4).

This book began its life several years ago when we both attended a conference at our alma mater, St. Patrick's College, Maynooth. There we bumped into the then editor of *Intercom*, Francis Cousins, who asked us to take on the writing of a series of reflections on the Sunday gospel readings, entitled "The Deep End." For more than ten years we have shared this ministry, endeavoring to offer a fresh perspective on each week's text. The reflections reach a wide audience thanks to their inclusion in parish newsletters and websites throughout Ireland and beyond. Recently, we were encouraged to put our reflections together to make them even more accessible, so we created this new resource that is now in your hand. While our original reflections were the starting point, in this book we have worked together to develop these further and to encourage the reader to engage more deeply with the word.

We are delighted that the timing of this publication means we are reflecting on Luke's gospel for Year C, for it has much to offer all who seek. In Chapter 5, Jesus urges Simon to "put out into the deep"—to cast his net out into the unknown. When Simon and the others do as Jesus asks, we read that they are "amazed" to bring in a huge haul of fish. Unexpected and abundant gifts are to be found in the depths when we are open to trusting and taking a risk. "Do not be afraid," Jesus tells Simon. We invite you now to come on a journey with us, to leave the safety of the shore behind and, through the story of Luke's gospel, to follow Jesus as he makes his way to Jerusalem. There will be many surprises and challenges as we travel through the year; Luke's Gospel is "an invitation that awaits a response." [1]

Guided by Luke, we aim in this book to explore how the gospel can open up new possibilities for how we live. We strongly believe that the Good News can speak to our human experience, that the word is truly alive and active (Heb 4:12), and that everybody's story is contained in it. It is powerful and radical, always pushing us to look with fresh eyes both inward at ourselves and outward at the world around us. The task of "interpreting the signs of the times in the light of the Gospel" [2] is as pressing as ever. We hope that *Delve Deeper* will help readers to integrate faith and life by putting themselves face to face with the word of God. The message of Jesus as presented by Luke has much to say to us. Our challenge is to see how this word speaks to us each week so that we can continue the narrative.

HOW TO USE THIS BOOK

The Church year begins on the First Sunday of Advent and subsequently moves through various seasons: Christmas, Lent, Easter, and Ordinary Time. Each year we focus on a particular gospel for our Sunday liturgies, following a three-year cycle. We read and hear from the Gospel of Matthew on Sundays during Year A, Mark in Year B, and Luke during Year C. Then, the cycle begins again. We also hear from John's gospel each year during Lent and Easter, and on some other feasts throughout the calendar.

So, welcome to Year C, where the readings are mostly taken from Luke's gospel, with the few exceptions mentioned above. The reflections in this book are designed as a companion for all those who would like to take a deeper look at the Sunday readings and explore how the gospel is relevant for our world today. They are short and accessible and can easily be read as a preparation for the Sunday liturgy, either for personal reflection or in a group. We also keep in mind all those who work in pastoral ministry who may also wish to draw on these reflections for use in various settings.

Each reflection begins with a reference to the gospel of the day. We highly recommend taking time to read the gospel text prayerfully before the Sunday liturgy (see the section on *Lectio Divina* below). Having prepared in this way, when we come to listen to the readings on Sunday, we hear the word in a very different way: bringing fresh insights and experiences with us. The reflections in this book could also be revisited during a quiet period later in the week.

Following each reflection, there is a "Go Deeper" section that suggests some steps we might take to live out the Sunday gospel more fully in our daily lives. As a companion to this book, we recommend that readers keep a journal where they jot down any thoughts that arise for them, including their responses to the "Go Deeper" questions. It is our hope that by the end of the liturgical year, readers will feel they have been on a journey with the Jesus of Luke's gospel and will be able to look back and see the fruits of this journey. As Pope Francis reminds us, "The words of the Sacred Scripture were not written to remain imprisoned on papyrus, parchment or paper, but to be received by a person who prays, making them blossom in his or her heart."[3]

LECTIO DIVINA

Lectio Divina means Sacred Reading. With roots that go into the Old Testament, *Lectio Divina* is one of the most ancient ways of listening for, and hearing, God's word in the Christian tradition. Thomas Keating notes that *Lectio Divina* has been the mainstay of Christian monastic practice from the early days. It consists of "listening to the texts of the Bible as if one were in conversation with God and God were suggesting the topics for discussion." [4] It is a personal encounter with God. It is not the intention of this book to replace this ancient spiritual practice of *Lectio Divina*; rather we encourage you to use *Lectio Divina* as a method of reading the texts that are proposed for each Sunday, either in a group or in personal reflection. After that, you can move into *Delve Deeper*'s reflections for each day. They are food for the journey and not intended to be a substitute for time spent with God's word. By setting aside some time—we suggest half an hour—each day, the fruits of this practice will grow throughout the week and across the year.

Much has been written about *Lectio Divina*, but we recommend the following:

Lectio (Reading): We *read* the text two or three times, not with the head but with the heart. We linger on the words, savor them, and gaze at the text, allowing ourselves to become familiar with it and the word to take root in us. What have we noticed? A word or phrase may have arisen. We repeat this word or phrase silently, like a mantra. In a group setting, people can be invited to speak this word aloud, without commenting on it.

Meditatio (Reflecting): This involves pondering or *reflecting* on the word. What light does what we are hearing cast on our lives (our relationships, challenges, joys) or on the world?

Oratio (Prayer): We may be moved in our hearts to respond through spontaneous prayer. This is our response to what we have read and heard. This is our side of the conversation with God. Through this process, as our prayer deepens, we begin to rest in God. The challenge for us is to allow space for this to happen, to discover the courage to let God speak in the silence, in the depths of our heart. It is a gift.

As we begin any spiritual practice, we may experience some resistance in the form of busyness or distraction. Bring this into awareness and gently name it. It may be useful to carefully consider your preparation for this time of encounter with God. For example, find a quiet place, set aside a specific time of the day, turn off your phone, and light a candle. Begin with mindful breaths, inhaling the peace of Christ and slowly exhaling any tension from the body. Do this ten times. Be aware of Christ's presence. Then begin your *Lectio Divina* process.

Through this ancient practice of *Lectio Divina*, we grow in awareness of Jesus alive in our hearts. We may feel an inner impulse to live out Christ's teachings in the world. Now is the time to turn to *Delve Deeper*'s reflections in order to break open the word even further.

LUKE WHO?

Before we begin, it is worth knowing something about our gospel writer, Luke. Biblical scholars estimate that Luke wrote his gospel around AD 85, so it is unlikely that he was a contemporary of Jesus. [5] He was an educated Greek speaker and a very skilled writer. Luke is often referred to as a physician (Col 4:14), and we are told he was a traveling companion of Paul (Philem 1:24; 2 Tim 4:11), so it is most likely that Luke wrote for a predominantly Gentile (non-Jewish) audience. The Third Gospel is not his only work, for he wrote a sequel known as the Acts of the Apostles. Luke is the only evangelist to tell us about his sources in the opening verses, where he says that they were "those who from the beginning were eyewitnesses and servants of the word" (Lk 1:1–2). Luke would also have had Mark's gospel (c. AD 70) as a source, and in addition a further source, labeled "Q," which is believed to have been used by both Luke and Matthew but has been lost.

Luke tells us in his opening lines that he writes for someone called Theophilus (Lk 1:3–4), who may have been a patron of his, and whose name in Greek, interestingly enough, means "lover of God." Whether Theophilus was a wealthy person who commissioned this work or not we don't know, but we can take his name to mean that Luke writes for all those who love God, "so that you may know the truth" (Lk 1:4).

WHAT'S LUKE'S STORY?

All writers bring their own slant to things, and it is the same with the gospel writers. They have different audiences, styles, and focuses, but the hero of the story is the same—Jesus of Nazareth. The gospel writers provide us with four different lenses through which we look at the Jesus story. From Luke's perspective, the theme of his gospel could be summed up as "The Great Reversal." In his writing, Luke comes across as someone who wants the door of God's Kingdom opened to everyone, which means overturning the unjust religious and political systems of the time. He sees hope for all in the message of Jesus. Luke sees the Kingdom of God present when all those who are on the outside of society experience inclusion as full members of God's people. Jesus was put to death, as Luke narrates it, because of his radical inclusiveness and compassion. In this account, Jesus is not afraid to touch those considered "untouchable" and to heal those in need of healing, no matter what religious law he is breaking (Lk 14:1–6). He describes God's Kingdom in parables, metaphors, and images—usually great feasts—centering his entire mission on bringing about its reality.

A note on language may be useful here. We have come to realize that the term "Kingdom of God" brings with it associations of empire and patriarchy. Various attempts have been made in recent times to address this issue, for instance, by referring to the Kingdom of God as the "Kin-dom" or the "Dream of God." Language will always be problematic and carry cultural baggage, especially when we are trying to describe something that cannot be seen in material form, something that is more a state of consciousness or a way of being than a physical reality. We use the phrase "Kingdom of God" occasionally in this book to stay faithful to the Scripture text, while also acknowledging the linguistic baggage.

Jesus' inclusive vision for the world and for each person motivates his entire mission. Jesus is clear that the Kingdom he speaks of does not only concern the afterlife; it is also something here and now, in this time and space. [6] Luke emphasizes that this Kingdom is not restricted to the confines of the Temple, the seat of power for the religious hierarchy of Jesus' day. It is far bigger than that, and this fact will be too much for some to handle.

We can tell an author's focus by noting what is unique to that writer, and it is worth remarking here that in all there are eighteen parables found only in Luke's gospel. These include some very famous parables, such as the good Samaritan and the Lost Son. [7] In these unique parables the focus is on compassion, forgiveness, and really *seeing* those whom society does not see. Luke gives a more prominent place than the others to the female followers of Jesus (Lk 8:1–3), especially to Mary, whom he depicts as the first disciple. Only in Luke's gospel do we hear Mary's Magnificat, where she proclaims that God "has brought down the powerful from their thrones, and lifted up the lowly" (Lk 1:52–53).

Jesus, for Luke, is someone who has come to deeply challenge people's expectations, who promises that the "last shall be first" (Lk 13:30), and brings "good news to the poor" and "release to captives" (Lk 4:18–19). As we journey through Year C, we are invited to hear God's voice within and find our way as followers of Jesus of Nazareth, cultivating inclusiveness, compassion, and a love that can turn the world upside down.

Advent

Introduction to the Advent Season

Welcome to the first season of the Church's year, Advent. In the Christian calendar, Advent covers roughly the four weeks before Christmas, starting in late November or early December. Advent, however, is not simply a countdown to Christmas. Rather, we might think of this season as a signpost, marking our path, lighting our way, pointing to something beyond itself. Yes, it is a time of preparation for our celebration of the birth of Jesus, but it also marks a new Church year and a time to start over in our relationship with God and with others.

During the next few weeks, as we dive into Luke's gospel, we will meet John the Baptist preparing the way for Jesus. We will meet Mary as she looks ahead to the birth of her baby, and Elizabeth as she welcomes and celebrates this amazing news. In many ways, these characters are an unlikely bunch—a marginalized, pregnant young woman; an older woman unexpectedly pregnant, and an eccentric wilderness preacher—but we read that they are all "filled with the Holy Spirit." They are the first witnesses to Jesus' coming into the world, and we follow their stories as they announce him to others.

During Advent, we are invited to a real encounter with Jesus. It is a time to wake up and to rediscover our joy in life. It is a time to practice the words of Mary, "Let it be," and to be open to what adventures may come our way. We become more aware of God's presence in the hidden places of our world, in ourselves and in the people around us. Can we be signposts lighting the path for others?

At this busy time of year, we are often caught up in the frantic joys, and sometimes struggles, of the season. The lead-up to Christmas evokes different emotions and memories for each of us. As we enter this new season and new Church year, it is important to take some time to check in with ourselves. The gospel texts for the next few Sundays offer us the opportunity to go back to the beginning and enter fully into these Spirit-filled days when the advent of Jesus, the light of the world, is so eagerly anticipated.

First Sunday of Advent

GOSPEL: LUKE 21:25–28, 34–36

Stay Awake!

As we take our first steps into Advent, the message is to stay awake! In today's gospel we meet Jesus toward the end of his ministry, instructing the disciples to be aware of the signs of the times and to stay "alert." It is a message designed to keep his followers on their toes.

It can be easy for us to fall into a comfortable rut, not really engaging with the wider world. When we do look up, we notice "the worries of this life": in the natural world, in troubled countries, in our Church, perhaps in our own families. But what would happen if we were to truly wake up? We can think of many people who are awake to the problems in society. One who comes to mind is Malala Yousafzai. In 2012, when she was fourteen, Malala was shot and almost killed on her way to school in Pakistan. She was targeted for campaigning for the rights of women and girls to education, a fight she continues today. She has said, "We realize the importance of our voices only when we are silenced." Another person who embodies this spirit is climate activist Greta Thunberg. Her "School Strike for Climate" began in 2018 with her sitting alone outside the Swedish Parliament. Since then, her protest has grown into a worldwide movement of young people calling for action to address climate change.

Both of these young women are "awake" to the world around them—their eyes are open, they see the injustices, and they have acted. They are forging a brighter future. Countless others are reaching out, speaking against injustice, and working to heal wounds in the natural world, in communities and families. We can't afford to sleepwalk through life when the gospel challenges us to be bearers of hope and good news. This Advent, we are called to be awake.

When we start to act, hope is everywhere. So instead of looking for hope—look for action. Then the hope will come.
  ♦ GRETA THUNBERG [8]

GO DEEPER

- As we begin this journey, think of a time when you felt truly "awake" to events around you. Can you become more awake to the gospel alive and active in the world?

- Awakening to the realities of the world or even of our own lives can be a painful experience. As Greta says, hope is found in action, in small steps. What small step can you take this week?

Second Sunday of Advent

GOSPEL: LUKE 3:1-6

Preparing the Way

Compare these two scenes. First, picture the flurry of activity that happens when a foreign dignitary—president, prime minister, or pope—visits your country. They are welcomed with a red carpet, leaders greet them, streets are cleared to whisk them to a reception, and they are given the finest accommodation with catering to match. Now, imagine an asylum seeker arriving at a port or airport. In Ireland, for example, they are brought to a reception center and then moved to a direct provision center to await a decision on their application—a process that often takes years. Yes, they have shelter and food, but they have limited freedom and few opportunities for involvement in society. The system has been rightly criticized as inhumane. This is just one snapshot of the unequal world we live in. Many people are denied the opportunities most of us take for granted. Those brought up in poverty, homelessness, war, or direct provision have a difficult road ahead. The system is stacked against them.

Today we meet John the Baptist, whose task is to "prepare a way for the Lord, make his paths straight," much as a messenger might do for a queen or king or some other VIP. John's was a radical voice, urging people to open their eyes and change their hearts. What if we changed our hearts this Advent by reaching out and removing the obstacles in front of people? What if we "prepared the way" for Jesus by smoothing the path for others, tearing down the walls of prejudice in our hearts and the walls in society that keep people apart, even one brick at a time? As individuals and Church, we can be the "voice in the wilderness" calling for and bringing about change.

> *What Jesus never said: "Feed the hungry only if they have papers"; "Clothe the naked only if they're from your country"; "Welcome the stranger only if there's zero risk"; "Help the poor only if it's convenient"; "Love your neighbor only if they look like you."* • JAMES MARTIN, SJ [9]

GO DEEPER

- John promised that rough paths would be made smooth. What are some of the rough paths in your own life? Talk to Jesus about them.

- A radical change of heart is needed right across society to honor the dignity of every person not just in words but in action. Consider some ways your parish could reach out to migrants, asylum seekers, and refugees in your community.

Solemnity of the Immaculate Conception

GOSPEL: LUKE 1:26-38

The First Disciple

The Solemnity of the Immaculate Conception celebrates Mary's holiness from the moment of her conception, "full of grace" and "blessed among women." This is a pure gift and demonstrates God's love for the human race gloriously at work. Mary must have treasured this gift, never to have felt separated from God's love and grace. This does not mean that Mary did not have to endure the struggles of life as all the rest of us do. In today's gospel we see her struggling with the angel's message.

When the angel Gabriel drops in uninvited to her and announces that she will carry a son, Mary's response is one of amazement: "How can this be?" She is right to be alarmed. Leaving aside the physical questions raised by the message, Mary knows that this is a situation that could bring social condemnation for her, even the real possibility of the death penalty. So, while we like to give Mary comfortable titles, let us not forget the challenge she faced at this moment as God intervened so radically in this young girl's life.

Mary will give space to God within her very body as she carries this baby inside her womb. She will give birth and breastfeed as a homeless woman in an animal shelter. Her Holy Family will be marginalized from the very beginning of this story. It is in this reality that God asks for space to dwell. We are reminded here of God's presence in the most hidden parts of ourselves and in the most broken parts of the world.

Luke places Mary in his opening chapter as a disciple. Even though she is initially disturbed by Gabriel's message, Mary questions, ponders, listens, and then responds with enormous trust, going out to proclaim God's word to Elizabeth. Mary does not know where her heartfelt "Let it be" will take her. It is a courageous move, one that will bring both joy and heartbreak. Mary, the first disciple, will stay true until the very end.

*Now I ask you: will you weave a body of humanness for me?
I need a tunic of humanness in which I can become one with
my creation. Will you make that human body for my eternal
presence? Will you give birth to my love, in your own life,
so that all creation might be restored to wholeness?*

◆ MARGARET SILF [10]

GO DEEPER

- Reflect on your day. Where was God present? When did you experience light, peace, joy? Was anything revealed to you today? In these Advent days, keep watch for God's presence in hidden places.

- Difficult decisions often require a struggle and, like Mary, we can become distressed. Sometimes a messenger helps us to discern. Reflecting back on these moments in your own life, when have you found this to be true?

Third Sunday of Advent

GOSPEL: LUKE 3:10–18

Quiet Joy

In today's gospel, John the Baptist cautions against the temptation to get caught up in having more than we need. If you have enough, share with others, he advises; do not charge more than your due, and be fair and honest in your dealings. His preaching leads people to question whether John himself might be the Messiah, but he sets them straight. He is laying the groundwork for Jesus, preparing the way for his radical vision of a world where justice reigns.

John's message is clear and practical and every bit as relevant for us today as it was in his time. It is easy for us to forget what is truly important when we are caught up in the merry-go-round of consumerism that pervades our world at this time of year; we lose touch with the heart of the season. By way of contrast, we should remember that for many people this is also a time of great generosity, with an outpouring of support for charity collections, appeals for food and toys, and ethical gifts.

Today is known as Gaudete Sunday. "Gaudete" means rejoice. It's an ideal time to recapture what Pope Francis refers to as "quiet joy"—the joy of God's love, of the blessings in our lives, of being able to share with others. It is a good time to take stock of how our Christmas preparations are going. If you are fortunate enough to have enough of everything, you might see a way to cut back on spending and donate some money or time to a favorite charity. If you are struggling with seasonal expenses, perhaps you might take a breather and consider reaching out for help. We pray that the joy of the gospel will fill our hearts as we continue our Advent journey.

> *Whenever our interior life becomes caught up in its own interests and concerns, there is no longer room for others, no place for the poor. God's voice is no longer heard, the quiet joy of [God's] love is no longer felt, and the desire to do good fades.*
> ◆ POPE FRANCIS [11]

GO DEEPER

- Take a break today from the shops, the lists, and the "noise" of media. Take a walk in nature. Rest in the quiet joy of God's love.

- "Whoever has two coats must share with anyone who has none; and whoever has food must do likewise." Consider how you can put these words of John the Baptist into practice this Advent.

Fourth Sunday of Advent

GOSPEL: LUKE 1:39-44

Pregnant with Promise

Who was the first evangelist? Does Mary come to mind? If we understand evangelization as spreading the Good News of Jesus Christ, we will surely recognize that the mother of Jesus was the very first evangelist—and a powerful one at that. She was the first to carry Jesus to others. When her presence prompted Elizabeth to be filled with the Holy Spirit, she became a model for all who seek to share Christ's light with others.

Over time, our images of Mary have become rather sanitized, partly due to cultural perceptions of the role of women but also due to the longstanding correlation in Church tradition between "holiness" and "purity" for women: "This highly symbolic figure, with practically all traces of humanity and womanhood removed, with no obvious sexual characteristics and no hint whatsoever of any female carnality, was exactly what the Church wished for women." [12] Today, however, we return to Mary's roots, to her early appearance as the brave, decisive, breathless, excited young woman who rushed to Elizabeth's house, pregnant with God's promise, pregnant with joy, carrying the Word of God, passing it on.

Many of us have a particular devotion to Mary. Advent is an ideal time to reflect on what Mary can teach us about being a disciple and "God-bearer" (*Theotokos*). God asks each of us to be bearers of God's love and Word. Our challenge is to create a space for God in all of our human experience, in our joy and in our brokenness. Let us follow in the footsteps of the first evangelist, Mary. Let us also listen to the experiences of the women in our Church and society who, through their strength and enthusiasm, continue the task of carrying Christ in and to the world.

> *The way to begin healing the wounds of the world is to treasure the Infant Christ in us; to be not the castle but the cradle of Christ; and, in rocking that cradle to the rhythm of love, to swing the whole world back into the beat of the Music of Eternal Life.* • CARYLL HOUSELANDER [13]

GO DEEPER

- Find some quiet time this week to reflect on Mary as an evangelist. Read the first chapter of Luke's gospel and follow Mary's journey. What stands out for you? What prayer arises in your heart?

- Does your parish make a conscious effort to genuinely listen to the voices and experiences of women and to involve women in decision making in a way that goes beyond mere tokenism?

ఌ 3 ఌ

Christmas

Introduction to the Christmas Season

F or the retail industry, Christmas usually begins some hours after Halloween, with an urgency and speed that try to skip the coming months and arrive at lighted windows and unrestrained consumerism. Let's not dwell too much on that here or get too involved with it "out there." In the liturgical calendar, the season of Christmas runs from midnight (or nightfall) of 24 December and continues until the Feast of the Baptism of Jesus.

During the Christmas Season, those of us living in the northern hemisphere tend to hibernate. The earth has tilted away from the sun and, even though the winter solstice has passed on 21 December, the days are still dark and quiet, the soil is resting, and our attention is drawn inward. Many people find winter difficult; indeed, with very little sunlight and the weather cold, it can be a tough time. But it is during these weeks that Christians celebrate something amazing: God literally entering into humanity, putting on skin and living among us as a full human person—in a way that we still find hard to put into words.

Jesus—a Palestinian Jew, who was born into a homeless family in an animal shelter in a remote part of the Roman Empire—was marginalized from the very beginning. Yet he is someone who transformed history and who continues to transform our lives today. Into all the harrowing struggles of our world, then and now, God is born. This is what these Christmas days invite us to contemplate and celebrate. Christ is born again each year in our hearts, if we can make room for him there, and in our world, if we look with awareness. As we light the white candle on the Advent wreath on Christmas morning, let us remember what it represents: the peace, unity, and hope for which the world desperately longs. Luke invites us to rejoice with the angels and the shepherds, joining together in praise, singing, "Glory to God in the highest heaven and on earth peace, goodwill among people."

A note on the texts for Christmas Day. In the lectionary, there are three different gospels which may be read on Christmas Day. At "midnight" Mass—known officially as the "Mass during the Night"—we hear the account of Jesus' birth, including the message to the shepherds (Lk 2:1–14). For those up bright and early on Christmas Morning, at the Dawn Mass we read about the visit of the shepherds to Bethlehem (Lk 2:15–20). The gospel reading for the Mass later in the day is taken from John's gospel (Jn 1:1–18). Since this reading is also used on the Second Sunday after Christmas, you will find a reflection for it on page 25.

GOSPEL: LUKE 2:1-14

Expect the Unexpected

Luke begins the Christmas story by setting the sociopolitical scene for us: Jesus will be born in a land ruled by the Roman regime where a census has been called. A census was not taken for the well-being of the people; its purpose was to enable tax and exploitation. It does not matter that Mary is heavily pregnant; she must travel with Joseph to his ancestral home, Bethlehem.

Luke only briefly mentions the actual birth of Jesus and the care Mary lavishes on him, before focusing his attention on the shepherds. There is a reason for their presence here. The lives of the shepherds would have been hard, full of poverty, fear, and struggle. So, the scene that Luke paints is not a tranquil setting: rather, it is a scene set on the margins. Everything about this story is provocative and uneasy. It is into this mess that God comes as a homeless child. We are being invited to expect the unexpected.

Luke begins his gospel as he means to continue: turning the world upside down in solidarity with the outcast. In showing angels rejoicing with the shepherds, he places the "highest" and the "lowest" together giving glory to God. The good news of Jesus' birth goes first to the marginalized. It is in their name that the shepherds are chosen.

As you sing the Gloria during this Christmas season, come back to this marginal space where it was first sung, with the angels and the shepherds in a field. There are no boundaries, only the promise of a deep peace for all, a peace for which the world longed and still longs. It is for this reason we rejoice. *Shalom.*

> *God is not afraid of new things! That is why [God] is*
> *continually surprising us, opening our hearts and guiding us in*
> *unexpected ways.* ◆ POPE FRANCIS [14]

GO DEEPER

- If this story tells us one thing, it is that God's self-revelation comes in the most unexpected places and situations: in a field rather than a temple; in a feeding trough rather than a palace. Can you recall an experience of finding God in unexpected places?

- The shepherds come in the name of all who are marginalized in our world, whose lives are full of struggle. We bring these people to mind tonight, in prayer before God.

Christmas Dawn Mass

GOSPEL: LUKE 2:15–20

Let Us Go Now to Bethlehem

Following their extraordinary experience with the angels in the field, the response of the shepherds is immediate: "Let us go now to Bethlehem and see this thing which has taken place." Their transformation has been caused by what must have been a deep encounter. Then, having arrived at the scene where they pay homage to the child, the shepherds do not keep this good news to themselves. We are told that they became preachers and that people were "amazed" by their words. Their journey did not end in Bethlehem; for them, this encounter with Jesus was only the beginning. Their lives were changed forever. We too are invited to this transformational space.

Mary's beautiful child, who has begun life in this world in the most extraordinary circumstances, is visited by these shepherds. What must Mary have thought? The text tells us that "she treasured all these words and pondered them in her heart." We are Christians because Christmas happened, because Jesus came to teach us how to live as good and compassionate human beings. This is why the shepherds rejoice, this is why Mary ponders. We are invited to Bethlehem, to allow this Love to penetrate our hearts. Like the shepherds, can we share this Love with those we meet? We might bring to mind all those mothers who bring children into the world under difficult circumstances: refugees, homeless people, women fleeing domestic abuse, women living in fear, women who carry the pain of institutional abuse.

Once the Love that comes into our world at Christmas is shared with others, *then* we can return, like the shepherds, "glorifying and praising God" for all we have seen and heard.

> *O Come, O Come, Emmanuel, come forth from deep within me*
> *with Christmas luminous beauty. For my heart has become the*
> *sacred crib, the birthing place of God-among-us.*
> ◆ EDWARD HAYS [15]

GO DEEPER

- Sometimes our life experiences are too deep to share with others, and we treasure and ponder them in our hearts like Mary. Words are not enough to describe them, and that is OK, for they become part of who we are. Reflect on these experiences this week. Smile deeply.

- Find space to sit quietly during these Christmas days. Try to become more aware of Christ present in your heart, the sacred crib. Repeat his name in your native language.

GOSPEL: LUKE 2:41–52

They Found Him in the Temple

Today's gospel is the only account in the canonical gospels where we get a glimpse of Jesus as a growing boy. Jesus and his family are on a pilgrimage to Jerusalem for the festival of Passover. As a twelve-year-old Jewish boy, Jesus is at the age when he is expected to begin taking on the responsibilities of an adult Jew. Here, we read that Jesus takes this commitment quite seriously, remaining behind to converse with the teachers in the Temple who are "amazed" at his understanding. We are not told anything further about Jesus' adolescent years, except that he "increased in wisdom"; with that observation, we can assume that he continued to ask questions, learning from wise teachers and observing the signs of his times. Jesus was not zapped with sudden enlightenment. He had to study, mature, and enter into deep reflection.

As a young person, Jesus is beginning to shape his identity. As with all families, this can cause difficulties. Parents want to protect their children, while adolescents want to explore and expand their horizons, and conflict often ensues. One must wonder if Mary's heart sank at Jesus' response to her, "Did you not know that I must be about my Father's business?" Today's gospel is a reminder of how helpless we feel at times, when we must let God's dream be dreamed in ourselves and in those we love. Mary has been reminded of the divine will that inspires her Son, and once again she treasures "all these things in her heart."

So, today as we celebrate the feast of the Holy Family, we pray for families everywhere. In all the complexities that life brings for families, may we be open to discovering God's path for each one.

Only God could say what this new spirit gradually forming within you will be. Give Our Lord the benefit of believing that his hand is leading you, and accept the anxiety of feeling yourself in suspense and incomplete.

◆ PIERRE TEILHARD DE CHARDIN [16]

GO DEEPER

- We give thanks today for the gift of our families, while acknowledging that family relationships can be complex. Bring any difficult situations to prayer. Ask for God's grace to enter and transform them.

- Sometimes we have to let people we love walk their own path and follow the way God has set out for them. Can you recall experiences of this in your own life?

Second Sunday after Christmas

GOSPEL: JOHN 1:1-18

Taking Root

We talk about having roots to describe a connection we have with a place or people. "Being rooted" or "putting down roots" means that we are part of something. It's a powerful metaphor from the plant world. The roots of a plant remind us of its relationship with its environment, and how it becomes part of the place where it is planted. We sometimes refer to an idea "taking root" when some thought becomes embedded in us, inseparable from our very selves.

The image of taking root is drawn from today's first reading, as is the image of making a dwelling (Sir 24:8, 12). These offer us a key to understanding some of the complex language of today's gospel, which is the Prologue to John's gospel. In its beautiful meditation on the Incarnation, we hear that "the Word became flesh and lived among us." The Greek word *logos* has a much richer meaning than is captured in its English translation, "Word." It refers to all-knowledge, all-being, that which is forever, the Divine energy, Creator of the universe, Being, Father-and-Mother of all things, God.

John tells us that this Word was with God, and was God, in the very beginning, at the heart of all creation. The wonderful mystery that we celebrate at Christmas is that this same Word is Jesus who becomes one of us. Jesus comes into the very world that came into being through him; he puts down roots in the world and in humanity. He is present in all people and in every created thing; he is at work in creation at every stage, then, now, and forever. It is a connection that cannot be severed, for the roots are too deep—we in God and God in us. God is not "somewhere out there" but right here, right now: our light, our joy, our energy, and our comfort.

> *God loves things by becoming them. God did so in the creation of the universe and of Jesus, and continues to do so in the ongoing human Body of Christ.* • RICHARD ROHR [17]

GO DEEPER

- The Prologue to John's gospel invites us to deep reflection. Read the passage a few times, savoring the language. Is there a word or phrase that stands out for you? Stay with this and allow God to speak to your heart.

- At the end of each day, ask yourself, "Where did I see God present in the world today?" How might a growing awareness of God's presence affect your words and actions?

Epiphany

GOSPEL: MATTHEW 2:1–12

We Observed His Star at His Rising

The Wise Men were probably astronomers and philosophers from the region of Persia, but most important of all they were seekers. They looked to the skies for astronomical signs that would foretell the birth of a powerful leader. They were awake to the signs of the times. One must admire these Wise Men for the way they set out faithfully on this determined journey, a journey that involved many risks. We don't know details of their religious affiliations, and it really does not matter, for this story of the Wise Men is the story of people of all cultures, all countries, and all faiths who make a journey in search of God.

Matthew sets their story in stark contrast to that of Herod. Herod is "greatly troubled" when he hears of a possible threat to his power. Rumors of a new king could potentially upset political and religious structures. Herod is an example of a narcissistic leader consumed by his own ego. In contrast, the Wise Men are humble and genuine in their quest to find this child who has been born.

The arrival of the Wise Men in Bethlehem is a moment of great joy and grace, as "on entering the house, they saw the child with Mary, his mother; and they knelt down and paid him homage." God is found in the simple spaces. Let us have the courage to take the risk and move out of our comfort zones in search of Jesus, just as the Wise Men did. They had no idea of what awaited them, but the gospel speaks of their delight and joy when they arrived at that place.

Christmas

> *We often make do with looking at the ground....I wonder if we*
> *still know how to look up at the sky? Do we know how to dream,*
> *to long for God, to expect the newness he brings, or do we let*
> *ourselves be swept along by life, like dry branches before the*
> *wind?* ✦ POPE FRANCIS [18]

GO DEEPER

• The word "Epiphany" (from the Greek *epiphainen*) means to
  shine upon or make known. Recall a moment when you came
  to a deeper understanding in your spiritual life or received
  a new insight—an "aha" moment. What "star" brought you
  there? What did you find there?

• The Wise Men find Jesus not in the halls of Herod's palace
  but in a stable. God is often found in simple places. When
  have you known this to be true?

The Baptism of Jesus

GOSPEL: LUKE 3:15–17, 21–22

Signposts

John the Baptist must have been a very dynamic and inspiring
preacher. He probably seemed a bit quirky, roaming around in
the wilderness, calling people to change their ways. The crowds
speculated "in their hearts" if John was the one they had been
waiting for, but he used all of this attention and popularity for
one purpose only: to point people to Jesus. There are many
people in our own lives who have pointed us toward Jesus,
perhaps by an invitation to an event or sharing with us a new
insight at just the right time: teachers, grandparents, religious,

inspirational speakers, friends... In them we see something special that makes us *wonder* so that our hearts are moved to *seek* a little further. They are the John the Baptists in our lives, signposts along the way.

Luke tells us little about Jesus' actual baptism except that he is baptized alongside "all the people." The account is centered on a powerful experience of the Spirit that occurs while Jesus is at prayer, and it marks the starting point of his ministry. The experience of being led by the Spirit is central to Luke's gospel. So far, the ministry of Mary, Elizabeth, John the Baptist, and others flows from an experience of the Spirit. The divine words experienced by Jesus tell us who he is, but they also invite us to remember who we are, beloved daughters and sons of a tender, loving God. God delights in us. God's love is not something we have to earn; it is a given because it is in the very nature of God to love. We are called to be ever aware of this dignity that is ours, to grow in awareness of our true selves.

> *The descent into the waters of our spirit, is a journey into the presence of divinity. Through immersion in waters of life there comes a realization that to be a child of the earth is to be a child of God....All human beings are children of God but not all live in the awareness that there is "that of God" within them.*
>
> ♦ W.L. WALLACE [19]

GO DEEPER

- Who has been "John the Baptist" for you in your life, pointing you toward a deeper relationship with Jesus?

- A meditation for this week: Repeat the last sentence of today's gospel, becoming aware of God speaking these words to you personally: "You,..., are my beloved daughter/son, with you I am well pleased."

❧ 4 ❧

Ordinary Time [1]

Introduction to Ordinary Time

W hen people hear the word "ordinary" they immediately think of something plain, unremarkable,
the opposite of extraordinary. We often tend to
think of "Ordinary Time" as a sort of "everything else" season—if it's not Advent, Christmas, Lent, or
Easter, it is "ordinary time." Yet we should not dismiss this
season or treat it as an anticlimax or downtime in between the
big feasts. The term itself comes from the Latin *ordinalis* meaning "ordered," so it simply refers to the way the Sundays are
named in a numbered sequence. The rhythm of the liturgical
seasons also reflects the cycle of life in the natural world and the
rhythm of our own lives.

During Ordinary Time we hear the stories of Jesus' life and
ministry through his teaching and parables, through his meals
and healings, through his conversations with followers and chal-
lengers, right up to his final journey toward and into Jerusalem.
Most of these accounts are of course taken from Luke's gospel

this year, and in following them we get a real sense of journeying with Jesus and of his vision of the Kingdom as a way of life, here and now. We notice again and again how Jesus turns the world on its head: associating with those considered sinners, inviting outsiders in, and preaching a radical new compassion. Luke also recounts several extraordinary miracles, indicating that the Kingdom is at hand. There is much richness to be discovered when we allow the story to unfold from one Sunday to the next. We are invited to be active participants in the gospel story, using it as a time to draw closer to Jesus and to grow and mature in our understanding and faith. Don't let this anything-but-ordinary time pass you by.

While defined as one season in the Church calendar, Ordinary Time is broken into two different periods. The first of these (Ordinary Time 1) runs from the Baptism of the Lord to the start of Lent, and the second (Ordinary Time 2) from just after Pentecost right up to the first Sunday of Advent, when the new liturgical year begins. Since the beginning of Lent varies from year to year, depending on the date of Easter, the number of weeks in Ordinary Time 1 and 2 will vary also. During Ordinary Time, we also celebrate a number of special feast days, which you will also find highlighted in this book.

Second Sunday in Ordinary Time

GOSPEL: JOHN 2:1-12

The Wedding at Cana

This Sunday we return to what the Church calls "Ordinary Time," when we read the accounts of Jesus' earthly ministry. There is nothing "ordinary" about this time, however, as it is during these weeks that we hear about all the *extra-ordinary* things that Jesus did during his earthly life. Today's gospel is one example. John calls this account a sign, something that points us to a deeper reality. In the Jewish tradition, a wedding symbolized the Kingdom of God, and Jesus regularly uses the image of a wedding feast to refer to God's dream for our world.

At this particular wedding feast, we are told that Jesus provides an extraordinary amount of wine for the celebration: "There were six stone water jars...each holding twenty or thirty gallons." This amounts to a minimum of 500 liters of wine or 600 bottles by today's measures. Not only does Jesus produce this huge amount of wine, it is also the *best* wine at the wedding. Sounds like a great party! In our reading, however, we might focus on the generosity of Jesus in this story, remembering that this wedding event is showing us something of who Jesus is, what the Kingdom of God is like, and how God operates in our lives.

In this story, the stone jars involved hold the water used in purification rituals at the time. This story, then, is a significant reminder of how Jesus can transform anything, including that which has become stale, into something that brings joy and new life, inviting people to dance and celebrate. This event was "the first of his signs, in Cana of Galilee, and revealed his glory; and his disciples believed in him." As followers of Jesus, we too are called to be agents of generosity, celebration, and transformation.

> *Transformation...begins with the people of God who start turning the things of death into things of life. And the kings and presidents and nations will follow.* • SHANE CLAIBORNE [20]

GO DEEPER

- When have you experienced great generosity? How have you been generous to others? Is there someone you can show generosity to this week—for example, with your time?

- What in your life needs transformation? Ask Jesus to transform that which has gone stale into "new wine," so that it can bring forth joy and celebration.

Third Sunday in Ordinary Time

GOSPEL: LUKE 1:1-4; 4:14-21

Jubilee

As is his custom as a Jew, Jesus attends the service at his local synagogue. Reading from the Prophet Isaiah, he tells the crowd that his ministry will be focused on opening people's eyes and freeing them from oppression. This is Jesus' manifesto, with its proclamation of "the year of God's favor." The reference is to the Jubilee year which, as we read in the Old Testament, was declared once every fifty years (Lev 25:10). It was a year given over to resting the land but also to restoring relationships between people. All debts were to be canceled, and there was to be a redistribution of wealth within the community. Jubilee, as a sign of God's mercy and justice, was meant to dismantle structures of inequality. It was a year of restoration, a chance to start again.

Jubilee, in that sense, is also the work of the gospel today. An example that comes to mind is the Black Lives Matter (BLM) movement, which started in 2013 in response to the shooting of Trayvon Martin and was most recently involved in protesting the murder of George Floyd by police officer Derek Chauvin. A poster that went viral read: *We said, "Black lives matter." We never said, "Only Black lives matter." We know that all lives matter. We just need your help with #BlackLivesMatter for Black lives are in danger!*

Jesus urges us to open our eyes to the oppression that exists within our society. It is there, even if it does not affect us personally. We need to be concerned with equality for women in Church, with the rights of LGBTQ+ people, and with all those whose voice is not heard. We are not short of injustices. Today's gospel is a blueprint for all those who consider themselves to be followers of Christ. Just as the Scriptures are fulfilled in Jesus' time, they must also be fulfilled in each of our lives.

> *Do something outside yourself, something to repair tears in your community, something to make life a little better for people less fortunate than you. That's what I think a meaningful life is— one lives not just for oneself but for one's community.*
> ◆ RUTH BADER GINSBURG [21]

GO DEEPER

- Where do you see "the poor" and "the captives" in your community? Pray about it. Where are you being called to act?

- Something to reflect on this week: When we come across an issue of injustice how do we respond? We come to know Jesus by following him, not simply reading about him. The gospel message challenges us to our core.

GOSPEL: LUKE 4:21–30

Isn't This Joseph's Son?

"No prophet is accepted in the prophet's hometown": this familiar saying comes from Jesus' words in today's gospel. We might find ourselves sympathizing with Jesus. No matter how much people have achieved in their lives, in their home places they will always be identified with their childhood selves and with their families. While this generates a sense of belonging, it can sometimes be stifling. There is always someone to ensure they don't get ideas "above their station."

Returning home to Nazareth, Jesus ("Joseph's son") at first impresses his former neighbors with his preaching, but as soon as he begins to challenge them, they turn on him. His message is a call to inclusion, a radical reversal of perspective, and they are so enraged that they hustle him out of town and attempt to throw him off a cliff. The carpenter's son shouldn't be speaking to them in this manner! This could have been a moment of grace for the people, if they were open to it, but it was hard to hear. Perhaps the implications of this Good News were just too challenging from one of their own.

We don't always recognize God's word. Sometimes it comes in unexpected packaging. As individuals and communities, we can be guilty of pigeonholing people, often silencing their voices. Do we listen to young people with their energy and idealism? Or the elderly with their experience and wisdom? Are we biased against certain groups of people? Do we shoot down the opinion of some people before they speak, just because we have disagreed with them in the past? When our hearts are open, we come to recognize the modern-day prophets who are bringing the dream of God to fruition among us.

Although they heard you, Lord, they failed to listen. They heard only what they wanted to hear. The truth hurt them, you made them feel uncomfortable, and they rejected you....Show us how we may seek your Kingdom and help to bring peace to a troubled world. • TONY SINGLETON [22]

GO DEEPER

- Jesus' message of openness and inclusion was too much for those who heard him. Jesus welcomed all. Do I welcome all? How does the gospel message of inclusion challenge me?

- "What do you think?" is one of the most important questions we can ask someone. When we really listen to the response, we learn and gain a new perspective. Try to put this into practice in the coming week.

Fifth Sunday in Ordinary Time

GOSPEL: LUKE 5:1–11

Into the Deep

The disciples are understandably skeptical when Jesus tells them to cast their nets "out into the deep water." They have been working hard all night and have caught nothing. They must think there's something in what Jesus says, however, or maybe they are just humoring him. Either way, they agree to try again. And what a result! They get such a huge catch of fish that their nets begin to tear as they fill two boats to the sinking point. They get a lot more than they bargained for, just by trusting Jesus and taking that leap of faith.

One line in this gospel that stands out is Peter's reaction: "Go away from me, Lord, for I am a sinful man." Peter is completely overcome, as well he might be. The scene makes him uncomfortable and painfully aware of his flaws, but Jesus immediately puts him at ease. Instead of focusing on Peter's shortcomings, Jesus looks ahead at what is possible for Peter, reassuring him with the simple words, "Do not be afraid." Peter has demonstrated his trust by being open to Jesus, and there are wonderful things in store for this disciple. A net full of fish is just the beginning.

We might never find out what's possible if we don't step outside our comfort zone, whether it's reaching out to repair a broken relationship, speaking up for someone who has been wronged, or taking the first step to change a habit that is destructive of ourselves or others. The big challenge is to trust that God, who is constantly urging us to pull away from the shore, knows what God is doing. God wants us to live life to the full, to take that next step we've been agonizing over. Do not be afraid; put out into deep water.

> *A boat is safe in the harbor, but this is not the purpose of a boat.* ◆ PAULO COELHO [23]

GO DEEPER

- Peter saw himself as a sinful person, yet God had great plans for him. Allow this idea to take root in you.
  Say: "God has a perfect plan for me."

- "Do not be afraid." In what areas of your life is fear holding you back? Reflect on the words of Jesus in today's gospel, and ask him to help you "put out into the deep water."

Sixth Sunday in Ordinary Time

GOSPEL: LUKE 6:17, 20–26

Blessed Are You

What's so great about being poor, hungry, or sad? On the surface, these Beatitudes of Jesus seem strange. "Blessed are you who are poor": surely it's better to be well off and well fed and to enjoy good times—or at the very least to be comfortable and content. Are these not the things we strive for in life? Jesus, however, is not interested in comfort or in maintaining the status quo. The Jesus of Luke's gospel is a revolutionary. He has come to turn the social order on its head: the last becomes first and the least becomes the greatest. His concern is always for the poor and marginalized. Jesus' vision is of a world where the unjust structures that cause poverty, hunger, and oppression are swept away.

Sadly, in our world inequalities are more pronounced than ever. Jesus challenges us to look around us. When he says the Kingdom of God belongs to the poor, Jesus is not only talking about the afterlife. He is also asking us if our communities, here and now, belong to the poor. Is everyone welcomed as a full member? Do we meet everyone's needs, or do some people go hungry, either physically or spiritually? Are we concerned for all, or only for ourselves and our own comfort? We are called to model our communities on Jesus' vision for our world.

Pope Francis has offered six "new Beatitudes" for the modern era. Like the teachings of Jesus, they remind us of the importance of recognizing the dignity of all and living in solidarity with those on the margins. Here they are:

Blessed are those who remain faithful while
enduring evils inflicted on them by others,
and forgive them from their heart.
Blessed are those who look into the eyes of the abandoned
and marginalized, and show them their closeness.
Blessed are those who see God in every person, and
strive to make others also discover him.
Blessed are those who protect and care for our common home.
Blessed are those who renounce their own
comfort in order to help others.
Blessed are those who pray and work for full
communion between Christians. [24]

GO DEEPER

- Read the Beatitudes in Luke's gospel, and think about how they might apply to today's world. Do any of the "new Beatitudes" of Pope Francis speak to you today?

- Our inner attitudes toward others shape our words and actions. Pay attention to how you see other people or situations this week.

GOSPEL: LUKE 6:27-38

An Eye for an Eye Will Leave the Whole World Blind.[25]

Turn the other cheek; love your enemies; treat others as you would like to be treated. These words from today's gospel are familiar, but they are among the most difficult of Jesus' sayings. Can we really be expected to love those who hurt us, to keep giving while receiving nothing in return?

The political landscape, particularly in the West, has shifted in recent years. We live in a time of upheaval and division. We are constantly encouraged to pick a side—right or left, liberal or conservative, pro-life or pro-choice. Every issue is divided into dramatically opposing views, with those on the "other side" labeled as deluded and out to destroy all that is good. The listening stops and there are only disdain and vitriol.

Jesus tells us there is another way. His words invert our usual human "wisdom" about enemies and forgiveness. In place of arguments and revenge, he proposes a radical new way of engaging with others. He is not encouraging us to be passive. Rather, he is inviting us to a "third way": to think about people not as enemies but as sisters and brothers, and to make a nonviolent stand when faced with persecution. We see the humanity in others, and we invite them to see our humanity in the way we treat them.

This approach can transform the world. People like Gandhi have shown what can be achieved by choosing a different path. Instead of meeting violence with violence, he and his followers engaged in peaceful resistance, and over time transformation came. Gandhi described nonviolent direct action (in Sanskrit *Ahimsa*) as "the greatest force at the disposal of mankind."

"Loving our enemies" is a call to constantly move towards restoring relationships.

> *I still find myself compelled by Jesus who was always subverting the narrative of "friend or foe" by saying "foe is friend"..."Who is right and who is wrong, God?" And God tells a story that makes it all a little bit more gray than comfortable—that challenges all sorts of listening ears.*
> ♦ BRITNEY WINN LEE [26]

GO DEEPER

- This gospel is extremely challenging. Let's not gloss over its difficult call to love beyond what we would imagine to be possible. Can you pray for someone who has hurt you or whose attitudes you find challenging? Send them peace.

- It is common for insults to be tossed around carelessly on social media. Examine your online interactions: just as in person, we are called to kind, respectful dialogue on social media.

5

Lent

Introduction to the Lenten Season

I n the past, Lent was often seen as a time to look down on oneself. Words such as temptation, evil, sin, and guilt were often dominant, leaving some people in darkness and despair. This was extremely damaging for many. Thankfully, today we are trying to let go of such language and see Lent for what it really is, a time for transformation and encounter. Indeed, for some people today, it is one of their favorite Church seasons. New Year resolutions are probably well out the window by the time Lent comes around, so in a real sense it brings us the opportunity of a new beginning, a chance to start again. Lent offers us a time for deep reflection, and for those of us who hear and read the gospel each week during this season, the texts offer a richness that can bring freshness to our lives.

Lent is a journey of preparation for Easter, a time to refresh our relationship with God, with those we love and cherish, with those we find difficult to love, and with God's creation. Lent is like a time of stocktaking: what's here that shouldn't be? What do I need to let go of? Where do I need to spend more time? The intention is not to beat ourselves up; rather, it is to set out on a journey that will help us live our best lives with our hearts open. This is what Jesus wants for us.

We read on the First Sunday of Lent that our first stop is the wilderness. Here we embrace three tools to assist us: prayer, fasting, and almsgiving. A suggestion for this season might be to spend more time with God's word, to give up some luxury, and to either donate what you can to your favorite charity or give your time to something or someone. These practices help us to focus and to grow in deeper awareness of what it means to be a follower of Jesus.

During this time, it is good for us to remove ourselves from our normal routines, to be still, and to stop and breathe. We need not be afraid of this, for the gospel shows us that time spent in the wilderness is Spirit-led and that we are not alone. We hope that you can use the following reflections to spend more time this Lent with God's word, in prayer for transformation, renewal, and encounter with the One who journeys with us.

First Sunday of Lent

GOSPEL: LUKE 4:1–13

Led by the Spirit

In today's gospel, Jesus is "led by the Spirit" in the wilderness. By definition, a wilderness is a place that is uninhabited and inhospitable. It seems a strange place for Jesus to begin. He has returned "full of the Holy Spirit" after being baptized by John, yet immediately that same Spirit leads him into the wilderness. Jesus is not left alone to be tempted; the Spirit leads him the entire time. The period of forty days reminds us of the forty years that the people of God wandered in the wilderness before they arrived in the promised land—"a land with flowing streams...a land of olive trees and honey" (Deut 8:1–10). Of course, Lent also lasts for forty days, a Spirit-led time when we undergo a process of renewal.

Luke places huge emphasis on the Holy Spirit. His is the only gospel where Jesus returns from his wilderness interlude "filled with the power of the Spirit." Luke uses this expression to describe "an emotional or spiritual fullness that overflows outwardly." [27] When Jesus emerges, he is ready to begin his ministry. The wilderness is not a place to be feared; it can be a place of transformation, a place where God is ultimately in control. It is a place of contemplation where we come face to face with God and with our true selves.

As we enter Lent, we hear the Spirit's call to trust. When we pause to take stock of the direction of our lives, we may encounter our own demons and temptations, but that is part of the process. Let us embrace this "wilderness" season as a time of genuine spiritual, and Spirit-led, journeying.

> *Our real journey in life is interior; It is a matter of growth,*
> *deepening, and of an ever greater surrender to the creative*
> *action of love and grace in our hearts. Never was it more*
> *necessary to respond to that action.* ◆ THOMAS MERTON [28]

GO DEEPER

- Lent is a time to discover where the Spirit is leading us. Set aside some time this week to consider how you will embrace this opportunity.

- The Spirit who led Jesus to and through the desert also guided him in times of struggle. So too with us. She moves in silent, unexpected and mysterious ways, awakening us. Be more attentive to her presence during Lent!

Second Sunday of Lent

GOSPEL: LUKE 9:28-36

A Transforming Space

Peter is overwhelmed, to say the least. It wasn't unusual for Jesus to go up a mountain to pray, but this time he takes Peter, John, and James with him, and what happens next is extraordinary. This vision of Jesus is like nothing these disciples have seen before, for they are given a glimpse of the glory of God. Is it any wonder Peter doesn't know what he's saying? This special encounter with Jesus only happens when they take a step away from their everyday activities. In this space, Jesus reveals his true nature to them. It is a dramatic moment, but it is also a moment of encouragement to spur them onward in their mission. The memory of this day will carry them and give them hope during the difficult times ahead.

Today we follow in the footsteps of Peter, John, and James, whose experience offers a fleeting glimpse of who Jesus is. It reminds us that there is more to life than our ordinary, everyday experience. Being a disciple means believing in this Jesus, the Son, the Chosen One. We listen to him even when, like Peter, we don't fully understand the meaning of it all, but are filled with wonder and hope.

While we may assume that this kind of "transfiguration" event is outside our realm of experience, life is full of instances where God "breaks through" into our world. The beauty of our natural world, the power of art and music to move us, the goodness and generosity of others—all these are moments of transformation when God reaches out to us. The more we tune in and spend time "on the mountain" in meditation and prayer, the better we will experience and appreciate God's presence with us.

> *Wherever you turn your eyes the world can shine like transfiguration. You don't have to bring a thing to it except a little willingness to see. Only, who could have the courage to see it?* ◆ MARILYNNE ROBINSON [29]

GO DEEPER

- Bring to mind a transformative moment on your faith journey. Perhaps someone gave you a new insight, or you had an experience that left you with a deeper understanding of God.

- The disciples in today's gospel "stayed awake" and therefore saw Jesus' glory. This week, become more aware of God's presence in your daily life. Open your eyes, ears, and heart more fully to the small yet real moments of transfiguration.

GOSPEL: LUKE 13:1–9

Gardening Tips

It is an age-old question: "Why do bad things happen to good people?" We hear of two tragedies in the gospel today. The first is where a number of Galileans were killed by the Romans as they made sacrifices to God in the Temple. Some Jewish leaders at the time viewed the Galileans as second-class Jews, and so the question raised here is about more than suffering. They want to know if the Galileans suffered because they were not really "Jewish enough." Jesus responds with a sharp question about another recent tragedy, when eighteen people were killed by the collapsing tower of Siloam. Were these people worse offenders than others in Jerusalem? Is this really how God works in our world?

Jesus then tells his hearers the parable of the fig tree. It is an appropriate parable for Lent, because it makes us a little uncomfortable by challenging us. Jesus invites his listeners to focus on living a full life themselves, rather than spending time wondering whether others deserve their misfortune. When we hear of tragedies it is often an opportunity for us to reflect on the big questions of life. It is also an invitation to ask ourselves, "How am I doing?", because we realize that death can come at any moment. In my life, am I bearing the fruit of which I am capable? The intent is not to beat ourselves over the head with a branch of the fig tree; rather, it is to help us live our best lives and to make the most of the time that has been given to us. If we are not bearing fruit, then we might take the opportunity of looking more closely at our lives to see what needs attention. Maybe some extra pruning or nourishment is required. The parable concerns the unfruitfulness of the tree, but it also suggests that there is the opportunity for change. Jesus invites us to the fullness of life.

> *"I wish it need not have happened in my time," said Frodo.*
> *"So do I," said Gandalf, "and so do all who live to see such times.*
> *But that is not for them to decide. All we have to decide is what*
> *to do with the time that is given us."*
>
> ◆ J.R.R. TOLKIEN [30]

GO DEEPER

- Using the analogy of the fig tree, reflect on what areas of your life need attention. What nourishment do you really need—for example, rest, prayer, company, exercise, or time in nature?

- What does fullness of life mean for you? Take time to reflect on this, using your journal.

Fourth Sunday of Lent

GOSPEL: LUKE 15:1-3, 11-32

The Elder Son

Sometimes we can be so familiar with a particular gospel passage that we switch off after the first few sentences. That would be a shame, especially when listening to today's parable, which is unique to Luke, and is one of the great blockbuster parables. The parables of things lost and found emphasize the unending forgiveness of God and God's rejoicing for those who return. Parables always have something to teach us. They enable us to engage at a deeper level with tough questions, inviting us to reflect on similar situations in our own lives. The main topic here is forgiveness, and the real challenge in the story is what happens after the lost son returns.

The Father's welcome for the younger son would have been considered extremely foolish by those listening to this story, and their viewpoint is mirrored in the reaction of the elder brother. After all, he has "worked like a slave" for years and is understandably upset at the lavish party that has been thrown for his delinquent sibling. The Father, however, reassures the disgruntled brother that his welcome for the younger brother does not change his love for him or diminish the inheritance he will receive.

This gospel shows us that God returns those who are lost to the community, regardless of the obstacles that we might put in place. Jesus teaches a lesson here in radical hospitality. No matter how far one wanders from home, God still loves us, waits for us, and is calling us back with open arms. The elder brother has a choice: he can come to the party or feel sorry for himself. It will cost him nothing to reach out to his younger brother, but his ego is in the way. What does he do? Significantly, Luke does not finish the story; rather he leaves it up to us to continue the narrative. We have nothing to lose in welcoming home the lost.

> *To forgive is to set a prisoner free and realize that the prisoner was you.* ◆ LEWIS B. SMEDES [31]

GO DEEPER

- Read the parable again and try to place yourself somewhere in this narrative: where do you stand?

- Forgiveness is a decision, but it is not always easy and can bring up difficult emotions. Bring to mind someone whom you find difficult to forgive. Send peace to that person or into that situation. Make this part of your regular spiritual practice if you can.

GOSPEL: JOHN 8:1-11

Another Way

The Old Testament law demanded that those caught in the act of adultery should be put to death. In today's gospel, we hear about a woman who has been arrested by the religious leaders and dragged before Jesus. There is no mention of her sexual partner—he may have been one of her accusers or a friend of theirs, but we are not told. This woman is being used by these men to trap Jesus as he teaches in the Temple precincts. Displaying the characteristics of a mob mentality, they want to judge, condemn, and even kill her. Jesus does not condemn the woman, of course, but a key piece of this passage draws attention to his demeanor. In the face of the fierce aggression of the mob, Jesus embodies a radical humility and remains calm.

We live in a stone-throwing society, one that cares little for the circumstances that lead people into their particular situations. We want someone to blame, and the sooner the better. If you watch the news, you will see the blame game in process daily. The mob mentality is contagious and often lazy, because it is the easy option when faced with complex circumstances. Those who accuse others often do so because they find inward reflection too difficult. Here, Jesus encourages the religious leaders out of that mentality and back to their own individual reality: "Let anyone among you who is without sin be the first to throw a stone at her."

Everyone makes mistakes, and we all need forgiveness from time to time. As we approach the Easter season, remember that Jesus can and wants to free us from these burdens and invites us to start again each time. This gospel also challenges us to relate compassionately to others. It is in this way that we can rediscover our common humanity.

I can hear the stones start to drop as the men walked away and soon the only one that was left with any right to throw a stone was Jesus. And he has no inclination to do so. We can see that the closer we are to God the less we want to throw stones at other people. • SHANE CLAIBORNE [32]

GO DEEPER

- Jesus calls the mob back to their humanity. In what situations is this call needed today in society, in the Church?

- Compassion is one of the many characteristics of a follower of Christ. How have people shown you compassion? Reflect this week on how you can be more compassionate to others.

Palm Sunday

GOSPEL: LUKE 19:28-40

Holy Holy

In this reflection we focus on Jesus' entrance into Jerusalem, which we read about at the beginning of the Palm Sunday liturgy. This whole account speaks to us of ritual: an occasion for praising Jesus, welcoming him, giving thanks for all that has occurred. For the crowds who gather it is a triumph; their Messiah has arrived at the center of their world, the Jerusalem Temple.

In Luke's account, Jesus goes ahead of everyone else, leading the way. The image of the colt is significant. Leaders of that era would enter into a city in a parade full of pomp and ceremony, on white horses with all the trappings of grandeur on display. We see this reflected even today, when dignitaries arrive in expensive jets or impressive limousines, stepping on to red carpets. These are all symbols of power, and Jesus' message deeply challenges those systems of power. His mission has been different from the start—a radical reversal, a lesson in expecting the unexpected. It was shepherds, not Roman emperors, who paid homage to him in the stable, and here he arrives in the holiest of cities on a donkey.

We are told that "the whole multitude of the disciples began to praise God joyfully with a loud voice, saying "Blessed is the king who comes in the name of the Lord!" This joyful hymn is the origin of the second part of the "Holy Holy" in our liturgies. We may well ask ourselves: Do we sing this as joyfully as they did, in gratitude for Jesus and for all the miracles in our lives? Their singing is an echo of the song of the angels as they rejoiced with the shepherds following Jesus' birth. Christ has come for all those who are marginalized in our world and to challenge the root causes of oppression. Luke's entire gospel has been moving toward this moment. The crowd is wildly excited. We know, however, how the rest of this Holy Week unfolds.

> *The story is still being lived today. Whenever people of faith decide to confront evil at its source, and do so with inner freedom, Jesus is once more entering Jerusalem.*
> ◆ MICHEL DE VERTEUIL [33]

GO DEEPER

- Don't miss the opportunity this Holy Week to read Luke's Passion account (22:14—23:56). Take a section each day or choose a character in the story to be with, seeing where it leads you. Yes, it is a long gospel passage, but try not to miss the journey that this narrative and this week offers.

6

Easter

Introduction to the Easter Season

Alleluia! This is a word you'll be hearing a lot during this Easter Season, which we are now entering. "Alleluia" is a Hebrew word meaning "praise the Lord." This tells us something about the focus of the season, which is characterized by joy and hope. Jesus has risen and he invites us into this new life. The Easter event illuminates our lives as individuals and communities, calling us to be light for the world.

The Season of Easter runs from the Easter Vigil to the Feast of Pentecost, a long period of fifty days. At this time of year, we are aware of the signs of new life around us. The days are longer and brighter, birds are singing, and flowers are blooming. The new life that bursts from the earth reminds us that God is the source of all life and goodness. Easter is a time of new beginnings.

Over the coming weeks, we take a detour away from Luke's gospel. We turn instead to the Gospel of John, with readings from his account of those who encountered Jesus after he rose from the dead, starting with the women at the tomb. We celebrate with these disciples as they are filled with joy at Jesus' presence, and we share in their struggles as they prepare to take their first steps as witnesses to the Good News of the resurrection. These disciples had a shaky start. They sometimes failed to recognize Jesus. They were afraid, they doubted, they hid. We can identify with their reactions. Sometimes it is difficult to see God at work in our lives. For that reason, the accounts that we hear over the coming weeks are very reassuring. Even when the disciples didn't realize it, Jesus was with them every step of the way. They were made new by his presence, and their fear was replaced by faith. When we meet the risen Christ, we are new creations.

The Easter message is for everyone, whatever our situation. It is never too late to make a fresh start. The good news is that Jesus is with us. He is present when we pray and when we struggle to pray, when we are happy and when we are hurting, in the beauty of our world, which is always being made new, and in the goodness and love we share with others. As we make our way through this new season, we open the door and invite the risen Jesus to enter.

GOSPEL: LUKE 24:1-12

Light Bearers

Our Easter vigil is the highlight of the Christian calendar, a night when we celebrate the defeat of death and the transformation of darkness into light. The Good News for us tonight is the same as that announced to the women in our gospel reading: He is alive! He has risen! In all four gospels, Jesus' female followers are the first to witness this extraordinary event. In Luke's account, several women—including Mary Magdalene, Joanna, and Mary the mother of James—encounter two characters at the tomb who break the news. But it is not until Peter sees the empty tomb for himself that he believes them. Commentators have suggested that the central role of the women is a sure sign that the resurrection accounts are authentic. At the time, women were not regarded as reliable witnesses, and for that reason their role would hardly have been fabricated. Luke acknowledges that, at first, their words "seemed an idle tale."

It is illuminating to reflect on this gospel today, when the Church continues to struggle to affirm women's dignity and authority as witnesses to the risen Jesus. These women were Jesus' close friends, supporting him all the way to the cross. At a time when women were marginalized in public life, God chose them as witnesses; yet the importance of this group has been neglected and suppressed over the centuries. Tonight's gospel shows us that God transforms all things, surprising us by choosing those we might least expect as messengers. What is God saying to us now?

In our Easter Vigil, we celebrate the victory of light over darkness. As we share the light of the Paschal Candle, we shine a light for all those who are not believed, whose words or roles have been treated as insignificant, who are discriminated against because of their gender, race, sexual orientation, or religion. We are challenged to see everyone as a person with innate dignity, bearers of the light of Christ.

> *We proclaim the Resurrection of Christ when his light illuminates the dark moments of our existence, and we are able to share that with others.* ◆ POPE FRANCIS [34]

GO DEEPER

- Where do you see female role models in the Church today? How might we better reflect the example of the gospel?

- At the Easter Vigil, we receive the light of the risen Christ from the Paschal Candle and pass this light on to others. Be conscious of the people around you. With deeper awareness, recognize them as people infused with the light of the risen Christ. Treasure this light within you.

Easter Sunday

GOSPEL: JOHN 20:1-9

A New Beginning

There is palpable excitement in the gospel passage we hear today. We find in it a lot of frantic running and breathless storytelling. Mary Magdalene rushes in a panic from the empty tomb to tell the others. Peter and John take off at a run, with the important detail included that John outruns Peter! Chaos reigns in their hearts as they look at the scene, until it dawns on them that Jesus really has risen from the dead. The empty tomb means one thing: Jesus is alive! Their despair quickly turns to joy.

Easter is a time for hope and new beginnings. Our celebration on Easter morning is like that first warm day of spring, when we throw open the windows and let the light and fresh air in. As followers of Christ, we share this morning in the energy and excitement of the disciples. Jesus has risen and life will never be the same. When the disciples enter the tomb, the linen coverings in which Jesus' body had been wrapped are empty and placed aside. It is a poignant sign that Jesus has left the bonds of death. In order to enter fully into the new hope of Easter, what are the burdens that we can leave behind in the tomb? Let the stone that has been rolled back and the linen wrappings represent all that prevents us from being free, all that keeps us captive emotionally, physically, and spiritually.

Our Church has not always communicated well the Easter message of joy. At times, it has been more inclined to place heavy burdens on people than to lift them into true freedom and fullness of life. Our challenge is to live as Easter people. With our joy and our passions, our loves and our desire to live life to the full, let us declare that Jesus is risen!

> *Decide in your heart of hearts what really excites and challenges you, and start moving your life in that direction. Every decision you make, from what you eat to what you do with your time tonight, turns you into who you are tomorrow, and the day after that. Look at who you want to be, and start sculpting yourself into that person.* • CHRIS HADFIELD [35]

GO DEEPER

- What makes you come alive? What is your passion and how might you use that enthusiasm and freedom to live life to the full?

- Does the Good News of the resurrection infuse every aspect of our activities as a parish? Are we a community of transformation, welcome, joy, and love?

Second Sunday of Easter

GOSPEL: JOHN 20:19-31

A Saint for Dark Times

Reading the news can be upsetting these days. It often seems that there is nothing but bad news. People are suffering across the world due to unjust economic systems and environmental degradation. Increasing numbers are homeless or living in poverty. Hateful rhetoric is becoming more widespread. We sometimes lose hope and go through shaky patches. We find ourselves asking: Where is God in all this?

In today's gospel we meet Thomas. As a disciple of Jesus, he has been through the mill. His friend has been brutally killed. The terrible suffering is still fresh in his mind. Now, the disciples' own lives are also in danger, so they are lying low. Traumatized and grieving, Thomas is not ready to hear the comforting words of his friends who say they have seen Jesus. His momentary wobble has earned him the nickname "doubting Thomas," and it certainly makes it easy for us to relate to him. When, an agonizing week later, he does finally encounter Jesus, we can sense his relief when he exclaims, "My Lord and my God!" The man labeled "doubter" now gives us one of the greatest expressions of faith.

We know life can be painful and messy, even unbearable at times. It is hard to hang on to our faith when we are grieving or anxious. Like Thomas, our trust can be shaken. Like the disciples huddled in the room, we can be afraid of what the future will bring. It can be difficult for us to accept assurances that God is with us. We may struggle to pray. We can become closed and isolate ourselves. Yet Jesus came among the disciples in their despair, calming their troubled hearts with his words, "Peace be with you." He came again to doubting Thomas, reassuring him with his presence. Thomas is a saint for those times of darkness. In our darkest days, may we encounter the healing presence of the risen Christ.

> *Life will always prevail, through all the layers of death in which we try to contain it.* ◆ MARGARET SILF [36]

GO DEEPER

- Recall a time you experienced tragedy or pain. How did you react? What helped to open up the doors that had become closed? Reflecting on such situations can help us when we next encounter tough times.

- Here is a meditation for this week. Find a quiet space and focus on your breathing. After some time, enter your heart and repeat the phrase, with Thomas, "Jesus, my Lord and my God." Stay with this for as long as you can.

Third Sunday of Easter

GOSPEL: JOHN 21:1–19

Come and Have Breakfast!

As in last Sunday's gospel, we are again with the disciples when Jesus appears to them. The scene is clearly set: by the Sea of Tiberias (or Galilee), Peter decides to go fishing, and a few others decide to accompany him. Now that they have seen the risen Jesus, we may find it strange that they are back to their day jobs. Perhaps they are unsure of their next step, wondering what Jesus expects of them. In the meantime, they have to eat and to earn a living.

Their night's fishing is unsuccessful. They are returning empty-handed when a stranger calls from the shore, advising them to cast out their nets again. This time, the catch is so great they can barely haul it in. Once the disciples recognize Jesus, he issues a simple invitation to come and sit by the fire for a meal: "Come and have breakfast."

This meeting takes place in the same location as the feeding of the five thousand earlier in John's gospel. The components of the meal are the same—bread and fish—and again a substantial amount is left over. As always, Jesus has provided more than enough. Through his death and resurrection, he has met their spiritual needs, though they do not yet fully understand that. Now, he meets their immediate needs by serving them breakfast in this ordinary setting and by being with them in friendship. He goes on to explain that following him will not be easy. His presence with them will be nourishment for the journey.

Jesus knows our needs. When we are disheartened or ready to give up, help can come from an unexpected source. It is often the simple moments of friendship and fellowship with others that are the most life-giving, when we sense God's presence with us, giving us sustenance for the road ahead.

> *For we are Easter people and we are called to celebrate the whole earth as the Body of Christ. Every act done in love gives glory to God: a pause of thanksgiving, a laugh, a gaze at the sun, or just raising a toast to your friends on your Zoom screen. The Good news? He is not here! Christ is everywhere and Love will make us whole.* • SR ILIA DELIO, OSF [37]

GO DEEPER

- The disciples were ready to give up when the "stranger" on the shore offered them a lifeline. Can you think of a low time in your life when help arrived unexpectedly from a stranger or friend? How did it change your perspective?

- Bring your reflection on this experience into your prayer. Jesus knows our needs and is with us today.

Fourth Sunday of Easter

GOSPEL: JOHN 10:27–30

Live Life

On this fourth Sunday of Easter, we hear a few short verses from the Good Shepherd Discourse of St. John's gospel. It is a passage that describes Jesus as the *genuine* shepherd who knows his flock and cares for them. There is a beautiful line in this passage that reads, "My sheep hear my voice. I know them and they follow me." Jesus knows each of us. He knows our deepest desires and our worries, fears, insecurities, and pain.

This should not disturb us; no, it should give us joy. Bring to mind your deepest friendships. What are the characteristics of such bonds? Usually, in order to know others really well, we must spend time with them, talking and sharing and listening to them. We become aware of their hopes and dreams; we find that we are extremely comfortable in their presence. These people are treasures in our lives, beloved soul friends, and we would do anything for them. Jesus, too, knows us intimately, and we are invited to listen for his voice and to know that we belong to him. This is a voice that brings peace, not discomfort or shame. It is a voice that says to us: I want you to experience the fullness of life!

In Jesus' time, being a shepherd was not a pleasant job, and there were many dangers involved. At night, shepherds would round their sheep into a pen and lie across the entrance in case they were attacked or stolen—literally laying down their lives for their flock. When things are not going so well in our lives, we may feel distant from others and from Jesus. Let this gospel be a reminder to us that Jesus is always very close to us, even when we feel abandoned. We can share our struggles with him, for "no one will snatch [you] out of my hand."

> *The beginning of the path to finding God is awareness. Not simply awareness of the ways that you can find God, but an awareness that God desires to find you.* • JAMES MARTIN, SJ [38]

GO DEEPER

- How can you come to know the voice of Jesus more deeply? One way is to commit yourself to spending some time each day pondering his word, using the practice of *Lectio Divina* (see page 3).

- A mantra meditation for this week might be to repeat these words, "Jesus, you are as close to me as my own breathing."

Fifth Sunday of Easter

GOSPEL: JOHN 13:31-35

Love One Another

To love as Jesus loved is the basic invitation of Christianity, yet we make it so complicated. The Greek word the gospel uses— *agape*—refers to a love of people by virtue of our common humanity. This can be challenging, of course, as it involves loving people we do not know and even those we do not like. Jesus came to show us how to live, and we can see in the gospels that Jesus loved all those on the margins of society, such as the poor, the unwanted, the sick, the lepers, and the convicts. Jesus' love was so inclusive that it eventually led to his death; it was too much for some people. Breaking through religious and political boundaries, this love threatened the unjust systems that kept the powerful on their thrones at the expense of others.

For too long, we really have not come to grips with the radical love of Jesus in the gospels. It is challenging to love those who are on the margins of our societies. We have only to look around our city centers or read our newspapers to become aware of those who are on the edge. To love as Jesus loved means to see everyone—refugees, prisoners, friends who have hurt us—through the eyes of our loving God. As always, we start with ourselves, acknowledging that we are infinitely loved by God. This can have a domino effect, resulting in an outpouring of God's creative love to those around us, and helping to heal and nourish our world. "By this everyone will know that you are my disciples, if you have love for one another." Let us dream of a world where this is a reality, and work toward making it happen.

> *The real, and potentially painful, questions will be, "How much love did I put into my work? What did I do for the progress of our people?...What real bonds did I create? What positive forces did I unleash? How much social peace did I sow? What good did I achieve in the position that was entrusted to me?*
>
> ◆ POPE FRANCIS [39]

GO DEEPER

- The questions asked above by Pope Francis are deeply challenging. Yet we need to face them. We all have circles of influence in our lives, our local networks. Reflect this week on your networks and how you are being called, as a disciple, to love as Jesus loved in these spaces.

Sixth Sunday of Easter

GOSPEL: JOHN 14:23–29

Shalom (שָׁלוֹם)

"My peace I give to you." The word for the peace in our gospel today is *"shalom,"* a Hebrew word used to say hello and goodbye in ordinary usage. Yet it also carries a much deeper meaning. *Shalom* signifies the peace that people long for, that peace that brings wholeness, completeness, and fulfillment. Jesus tells us that this *shalom* is a peace that the world does not give. It comes through cultivating a deep awareness of the Divine Spirit within our hearts, "our home." This is the true peace we long for, but there are many obstacles and distractions in our way.

For example, one of the causes of the ecological crisis our world is currently facing is over-consumption. In *Laudato Si'*, the encyclical of Pope Francis on the environment, he notes that the roots of this crisis are deeply spiritual. We are constantly trying to bring fulfillment to our lives by having the next upgrade, the next new gadget. This over-consumption is driven by the market, but it only succeeds because we are not at peace with ourselves. Goods are marketed to fill a gap, which they never can fill. At its heart, unbridled consumerism is driven by a lack of peace. In contrast, the peace that Christ offers is freely given, waiting for our acceptance. It comes from a loving interior relationship with God, which brings with it wholeness and peace.

> *When we understand the essential unity of all that is, we discover the possibility of "peace"—the kind of peace that in Hebrew is called **Shalom**, which is infinitely more than an absence of strife; it is the wholeness of the web of life itself and of every creature in it, held in the wholeness of the one God.*
>
> ✦ MARGARET SILF [40]

GO DEEPER

- Do you over-consume? Impulse buying is something we all do from time to time. When shopping, try to do so with greater awareness: Do I really need this item? Where was it made? Will it bring me the peace I am really searching for?

- Create space for meditation this week, beginning with five minutes each day. Focus on your breath. Use the mantra *Shalom*. As you inhale, silently say *"Sha-"* and as you exhale *"lom."* Bring awareness to your heart and visualize Christ seated there. *Shalom.* Try to bring this into your daily spiritual practice.

GOSPEL: LUKE 24:46-53

Easter People

Today we read the story of Jesus' Ascension from the final verses of Luke's gospel. Luke also writes about this event in the Acts of the Apostles. In that account, the disciples are asked a question, "Men of Galilee, why do you stand looking up toward heaven?" (Acts 1:11). If we only look skyward for the risen Christ, we lose sight of the reality of his presence all around us, in every person, in each created thing, in the web of life.

It is interesting that the disciples return to Jerusalem after the Ascension "with great joy." One might expect them to be full of sorrow, yet they are not. They know that nothing can be as it was before, and that they can no longer return to their former lives. The resurrection has changed everything.

And so it is for us. The Easter story continues, because as Christians we live with an assurance that pain, grief, and death will not have the last word. Christ has shown us that the story does not end here, and so we can dare to shine the light of hope and wholeness into the empty tomb, into the darkest of situations. Hope lives.

The disciples are sent out to carry Christ's message of love and forgiveness into the world. There will be many challenges for them. We are also called to be Easter People, carriers of this Easter message, active in the world. Easter brings a joy and hope that we can share, so that people are not left only "looking upward" for the risen Christ but can also see Christ radiated in the world around them.

> *God has given us the power to create beauty, to make another smile, to be a healing presence in someone's sorrow, to bring justice to the oppressed, to console those in difficulty, to bring peace and joy to others, to help those in need, to laugh and enjoy life, to do good and turn from evil, to forgive those who have hurt us, and, most of all, to love.* ◆ IRIS PEREZ [41]

GO DEEPER

- Easter People are everywhere. They shine light into dark situations. Where have you encountered such people in your own life? When have you shone that light of hope for others?

- Where do you see the risen Christ in the world today, in creation, in people, in community spirit?

Pentecost Sunday

GOSPEL: JOHN 20:19–23

Peace Be with You

We read today that the disciples are locked away in a house. Fear has gripped them. Their friend has been killed, their hopes and dreams have been shattered, and now they fear for their own lives. This scene takes place after Mary Magdalene has already told them that she has seen the risen Jesus, but they don't believe her. The disciples remain closed.

There are times in our own lives when we, too, isolate ourselves, and other times when we have no choice but to do so. One only has to recall the COVID-19 pandemic that began in 2020. At the beginning of that year, no one could imagine the way the pandemic would unfold across the world: the rapid spread of infection, the staggering death toll, overburdened hospitals, the world in lockdown, businesses closed. In the first weeks of social distancing many people were in shock, and this shock would soon turn to anxiety and fear. Many vulnerable people were left alone and afraid. We experienced a collective grief as this new reality unfolded.

Today's gospel reminds us that dark situations can be transformed. During the pandemic, we witnessed many extraordinary acts of kindness and generosity. Think of the heroes on the front line who put their lives at risk for those suffering, or the good neighbors and friends who reached out to one another. These rays of light help us to remember that the Spirit is constantly at work in this world, transforming situations, moving us to act in spaces that seem hopeless. Any period of isolation can be tough, but it can also be an opportunity to take stock, to think about what kind of world we want to live in and how we can contribute to the emergence of that world. One does not emerge from a crisis unchanged. The risen Christ *breathes* the Spirit into our lives continuously, offering us peace—*Shalom*—and the opportunity for renewal.

> *Historically, pandemics have forced humans to break with the past and imagine their world anew. This one is no different. It is a portal, a gateway between one world and the next. We can choose to walk through it, dragging the carcasses of...our dead ideas, our dead rivers and smoky skies behind us. Or we can walk through lightly, with little luggage, ready to imagine another world.* • ARUNDHATI ROY [42]

GO DEEPER

- Pentecost transformed the disciples. Can you remember any experience in your own life that transformed you in some way? How have you emerged from the "portal" of the pandemic? What signs of renewal have you seen in your world?

- A mantra for this week: in meditation, repeat the words, "Come, Holy Spirit."

Trinity Sunday

GOSPEL: JOHN 16:12-15

The Spirit Will Guide

In today's gospel, we see that Jesus is comfortable with an element of mystery. Speaking to the disciples before his arrest, Jesus is preparing them for the gift of the Spirit. The word he often uses is "Advocate," meaning helper or comforter, indicating that the disciples will not be left to struggle on alone. We hear Jesus say that the complete truth is too much for the disciples now. The mysteries of his life, death, and resurrection—and the implications they will have for his followers—all will become clearer in due course. The Spirit will guide them, he says.

Down through the years, the Church has attempted to put words on this great mystery of the Trinity. It was three hundred years after Jesus' death before the Church spoke officially of God as One in three Persons. A great deal has been written about this mystery since then. In recent times, C.S. Lewis described God as "a dynamic, pulsating activity, a life, almost a kind of drama. Almost...a kind of dance." [43] As Jesus told the disciples, not everything is revealed at once. The Spirit is still at work among us, like a dynamic activity or dance. The beauty of creation is constantly unfolding in front of our eyes. Thanks to the gift of science, we are discovering amazing things about our planet, our universe, our bodies, and our minds. As humanity, as Church, and as individuals, our journey continues, with the Spirit gradually unveiling God's message for our place and time. We don't yet have all the answers about this beautiful life. Our task is to listen and be awake to the many ways God speaks to us and calls us into the life of God.

> *"Circling around" is all we can do. Our speaking of God is a search for similes, analogies and metaphors. All theological language is an approximation, offered tentatively in holy awe. That's the best human language can achieve....We are in the realm of beyond, of transcendence, of mystery.*
> ◆ RICHARD ROHR [44]

GO DEEPER

- The world reveals greater meaning over time. Science has shown us that each event in creation could not have happened without that which went before it. Looking back at events in your life, even sad or difficult ones, where have you found this to be true?

- The Spirit is that life-giving force that animates our world. She inspires and energizes. Where do you see this energy and creativity in your own life and in your community?

Corpus Christi

Gift of Love

In today's gospel, we meet Jesus who is with people who are in need. The crowds have followed him to a deserted place, and it is now nearing nightfall. If Jesus is to send them away, as the disciples recommend, the people will likely go hungry as they make their way to find shelter for the night. Instead, he directs the disciples to "give them something to eat." When they object that they have only meager provisions, Jesus uses what they have to pull off a remarkable feat—a feast for the crowd.

This passage recalls several Old Testament stories about God providing for God's people. We remember, for instance, how the Israelites were fed in the desert (Ex 16:1-18), and how Elisha fed a crowd in time of famine (2 Kg 4:42-44). Today, it brings to mind the situation of migrants and asylum seekers across the world, people who experience hardship and often mistreatment at our borders. The gospel leaves no doubt about our obligation to protect them, just as Jesus provided for the hungry crowds. Today's gospel also echoes the Eucharistic meal, with Jesus taking the bread, blessing it, and having the disciples distribute it. With these words, Luke is clearly marking the links between the Eucharist and practical care for all those in need.

Jesus doesn't produce this meal from nothing. He transforms what the disciples have into a blessing for many. Sharing in the Eucharist means sharing our resources. It means ensuring people are not left to fend for themselves in crisis situations. When we receive the Body of Jesus in the Eucharist, it is a gift of love. But if we do not give in return, we are wasting the gift. Where people are hungry, homeless, or mistreated, it is our responsibility, as followers of Jesus, to share and to provide.

In the Eucharist, Jesus becomes the voice of those who have no voice. He speaks for the powerless, the oppressed, the poor, the hungry. In fact, he takes their place. And if we close our ears to their cries, we are shutting out his voice too.

♦ PEDRO ARRUPE, SJ [45]

GO DEEPER

- When the disciples wanted to send people away, Jesus made them welcome. Who is being sent away from our celebration of Eucharist today? How can we welcome them?

- No matter how little we think we have to give, God will provide beyond our imagining, but we are invited to take the first step. Think about how you can put more of your time or resources at the service of others, particularly those in crisis.

❧ 7 ❧

Ordinary Time [2]

Eighth Sunday in Ordinary Time

GOSPEL: LUKE 6:39–45

Can the Blind Lead the Blind?

In today's gospel, Jesus is teaching "a great multitude of people from all of Judea" who have come to hear him (Lk 6:17). He reminds the disciples that if they are to teach others, then they must first be students who have learned to imitate their Teacher; otherwise, everyone will end up in the ditch. This is also a reminder to each of us to remain close to Jesus so that we are continuously nourished and taught by him.

There is another warning in this text too: against hypocrisy. In an almost hilarious image, Jesus warns his opponents not to miss the log in their own eye when they point out the speck in someone else's eye. The lesson is clear: we must begin with ourselves. In the encyclical *Fratelli Tutti*, Pope Francis speaks about universal love, noting that it is much more than just a nice concept. Universal love involves loving actual human beings, in all their messiness and brokenness. We are urged to stop and think before we make harsh comments about others or pass judgment on them, because we never really know what is going on in another person's life. There is also the real possibility that the faults we find in others are mirroring something that we need to pay attention to in ourselves. The call is to interiority and a reminder of our common humanity.

The final part of this gospel speaks to us about what fills our hearts. If the media we consume is littered with fake news, bitterness, suspicion, and hatred, then this is probably what we are cultivating in ourselves. On the other hand, if we spend time with the Teacher, where we experience healing, learn to forgive, and listen to another's point of view, then our hearts will cultivate universal love. "For it is out of the abundance of the heart that the mouth speaks."

> *Come, Holy Spirit, show us your beauty, reflected in all the peoples of the earth, so that we may discover anew that all are important and all are necessary, different faces of the one humanity that God so loves. Amen.* ◆ **POPE FRANCIS** [46]

GO DEEPER

- This week, pay more attention to what you feed your mind and heart. Are you nourishing your whole self in a positive way? What spiritual practices do you have that help you to learn from Jesus, the Teacher?

- Universal love involves loving people in all their brokenness. Who are those you find difficult to love? Send them peace.

Ninth Sunday in Ordinary Time

GOSPEL: LUKE 7:1–10

Not Worthy

Centurions were army officers who commanded a hundred soldiers. In Jesus' time, they were part of the regime that oppressed the Jewish people. Today's gospel concerns a centurion who appears to be a good character. His servant is sick, so he sends some local elders to Jesus asking for help. These elders are well intentioned as they approach Jesus, appealing to him because, they argue, the centurion is "worthy" and "loves our people." In practice, however, these elders are putting limits to God's love. In making a special case for this centurion, they are implying that his sort wouldn't normally merit help.

This is not how Jesus operates. While the intercessors provide a checklist of the centurion's worthy qualities, Jesus simply sees a person in need of help. In fact, he is "amazed" at the centurion's faith. This word only occurs one other time in Luke's gospel—when Jesus visits his hometown of Nazareth and is "amazed" at their *lack* of faith (Lk 14:14–30). The humility of the centurion, who considers himself not worthy to have Jesus enter his house, contrasts with the attitude of the elders. Yet the centurion has utter confidence in Jesus: "Only speak the word, and let my servant be healed."

Jesus is addressing our preconceived beliefs about who is worthy of our time, or of God's time. We are invited to examine our attitudes, uncomfortable though that may be. Is it our place to judge who is worthy, who is included in our community, who can receive the sacraments? Only God knows what is in a person's heart, and God's love cannot be earned. It is freely given, and the centurion understands this.

> *Everyone can share in some way in the life of the Church; everyone can be part of the community, nor should the doors of the sacraments be closed for simply any reason....The Eucharist, although it is the fullness of sacramental life, is not a prize for the perfect but a powerful medicine and nourishment for the weak.* ◆ POPE FRANCIS [47]

GO DEEPER

- Every time we receive the Eucharist, we echo the words of the centurion, "I am not worthy that you should enter under my roof." Next time you approach communion, do so with the knowledge that Jesus' gift of himself is freely given, not earned.

- Jesus welcomed everyone to the table and did not refuse anyone. What is his treatment of the centurion saying to us today in relation to how we celebrate and live the Eucharist?

Tenth Sunday in Ordinary Time

GOSPEL: LUKE 7:11–17

Gut Feeling

We sometimes use physical imagery to describe our reaction to a sad situation. Our "heart goes out" to someone who is suffering, we say, or we find something to be "gut-wrenching." In today's gospel, Luke tells us that Jesus "had compassion" for the widow burying her son. The Greek term (*esplanchnisthe*) describes a very physical reaction: a "turning over of the insides" with compassion. This expression only occurs in two other places in Luke: in the parables of the good Samaritan (Lk

10:33) and the prodigal son (Lk 15:20). It is usually translated as "felt sorry" or "moved with pity," but these expressions don't capture the depth of the emotion evoked. When Jesus identifies with a hurt person, his entire being is affected, resulting in an outpouring of love. Apart from her grief as a mother, the woman in today's gospel has been left without any other family and is at risk of losing her economic security, even the roof over her head. Her situation touches the very heart of Jesus. He feels her grief in a physical way.

We feel something like this when we encounter suffering. You may recall the shocking image that emerged on 2 September 2015 of a three-year-old Syrian boy found dead on a beach in Turkey. His name was Alan Kurdi, and he, along with his brother and mother, drowned after fleeing their home. All who saw the photo were deeply moved, and for a time the sight ignited an outcry about the refugee crisis. Regrettably, many of the promises to act have since been forgotten. Jesus' response to the widow in the gospel today is to act immediately. This gut-wrenching reaction to suffering is true compassion. It is the force that compels us to reach out to others, to feel their pain and to act on it.

> *I saw the suffering and I let myself feel it....I saw the injustice and was compelled to do something about it. I changed from being a nun who only prayed for the suffering world to a nun with my sleeves rolled up, living my prayer.*
> ◆ SR. HELEN PREJEAN [48]

GO DEEPER

- Think of a time when you really felt for someone, experiencing a "turning over of the insides." How did you respond? It may have been in prayer or action. Sometimes all we need to do is be present.

- Recall a time when you were in pain or suffering. Who reached out to you? Know that Jesus feels a depth of compassion for us and is with us always.

Eleventh Sunday in Ordinary Time

GOSPEL: LUKE 7:36—8:3

Celebrate Mercy

In today's gospel, Jesus has been invited to dine at the house of Simon the Pharisee. As expected, Simon keeps to the strict guidelines concerning meals and ritual purity. Women are not permitted to take part, but suddenly an unwanted guest arrives. We are told nothing of this woman's past, except that she was a "sinner," suggesting that she is carrying some burden from which she wishes to be free. She knows exactly where to go: to Jesus. This woman has to cross many social barriers to get to Jesus, but she is clearly determined. She is ready to receive God's grace and able to celebrate it. This is in contrast to the others present, who find it difficult to comprehend a God who accepts sinners. Their hearts are closed. They are unable to celebrate as she does, joyfully and extravagantly. Mercy is what keeps us available to one another and opens our heart to strangers. "It is the glue of the human race." [49] Let us join with this woman in her beautiful celebration of mercy.

The last lines of the gospel remind us of the prominent role of the women who journey with Jesus. Luke refers to some of them by name: Mary Magdalene, Joanna, and Susanna. These are the same women who will be present at Jesus' burial and will be witnesses to his resurrection. They are key members of Jesus' community of disciples, yet their stories have, for the most part, been written out of history. We celebrate mercy today, thanks to the powerful witness of the woman in the gospel text. Let us also celebrate the women who were included in Jesus' earthly community, who provided for him, and who stayed with him until the very end. They were the first to bear witness to the resurrection and to preach this foundational event of Christianity.

> *The spiritual life of a woman never knows total maturation in an environment that never seeks her opinions, her interpretations, her insights and her experience of God. Whatever ministry she was born to perform never comes to light, is lost to the Church, dies on the vines that were never cultivated.* • JOAN CHITTISTER [50]

GO DEEPER

- Sometimes the hardest thing is to forgive ourselves; the emotions involved can be complex. When have you found this to be true? Can you celebrate forgiveness this week in gratitude for God's grace in your life?

- The women mentioned in the gospel today were clearly part of Jesus' close circle. What is this saying to a patriarchal Church today, 2,000 years later?

Twelfth Sunday in Ordinary Time

GOSPEL: LUKE 9:18–24

But You...

Today's passage marks a turning point in Luke's gospel. When Peter declares Jesus as the Messiah, Jesus immediately follows by predicting his suffering and death. We are not told how the disciples react, but it can't be easy for them to hear. Soon afterward, Jesus invites Peter, John, and James to witness the Transfiguration (Lk 9:28–36), when Jesus' true nature will be revealed to them. What a strange journey for Peter! In today's gospel, Peter is correct when he says that Jesus is "the Messiah of God," but Jesus then makes it clear that he is not the mighty political figure they were expecting. Jesus wants them to realize that being the Messiah means that he will be rejected and put to death. Not only that, but his followers must prepare for a similar fate: they too will have a heavy cross to bear. It's a disturbing vision of discipleship, a warning of what is to come. But it will not end in death. Jesus will be raised from the dead, and the disciples will share in that life also.

Our vision of God informs how we live. When Peter recognized Jesus as the Messiah, there were implications for living. Jesus asks us the question he asked his disciples: "Who do you say that I am?" Like Peter, we may know the answer in theory, but are we prepared to examine what it might mean to take up our cross and follow him? We answer the question about Jesus by our actions, by our willingness to be selfless and to lead a life of service as Jesus did. Can I give up my time to help others? Can I forgo purchasing a luxury item and donate to charity instead? Can I risk my reputation by standing up for someone who is mistreated? Can I show kindness always, even when it is challenging?

> *The fiery energy of God that so burns inside us will come to maturity, creativity and calm when we shape our lives and our bodies in the way that Jesus shaped his, when we help him carry the Incarnation forward.* ◆ **RONALD ROLHEISER** [51]

GO DEEPER

- "Who do you say that I am?" In prayer, talk to Jesus about who he is for you—friend, beloved, healer. Or does another word or phrase arise for you?

- Jesus' leadership is not what the disciples expected. It is a peace-filled leadership in solidarity with those who are oppressed. Who in today's society models this way?

Thirteenth Sunday in Ordinary Time

GOSPEL: LUKE 9:51–62

The Way

We read today from the beginning of the central section of Luke's gospel, which is primarily concerned with Jesus' journey to Jerusalem (Lk 9:51—19:27). The time for Jesus to "set his face toward Jerusalem" has arrived. The narrative takes on a solemn tone, depicting Jesus' determination but also anticipating the challenges that lie ahead. It will not be a straight path for the Jesus community. There will be hospitality along the road, but it will also involve rejection and struggle.

The way to Jerusalem is symbolic of the Christian journey, and indeed the early Christian movement was known as "The Way." [52] This is a term sometimes used today to refer to the famous pilgrimage route to Santiago de Compostela in the north of Spain. Anyone who has walked the Camino knows what a deeply spiritual experience it can be. Yes, there are blisters, aches, and pains, stifling heat, and not-so-comfortable sleeping conditions, but it is also a road of discovery, friendship, prayer, hospitality, and solidarity. There is something very transformative about walking day after day. The body becomes attuned to the earth. You engage on a different level with nature, villages, communities, changing landscapes, new faces—and ultimately with Christ who dwells within. Few people are the same after this experience. For the disciples, this will certainly be true of their journey.

At the end of the text, Jesus' words to the one who wishes to join them may seem harsh. Why couldn't this person be allowed to wrap up loose ends before embarking on the Way? Jesus' call is one that radically uproots people; it is a difficult walk that should deeply challenge us if we are really living the message of the gospel. *Buen Camino*.

> *Part of what makes roads, trails and paths so unique as built structures is that they cannot be perceived as a whole all at once by a sedentary onlooker. They unfold in time as one travels along them, just as a story does as one listens or reads, and a hairpin turn is like a plot twist.* • REBECCA SOLNIT [53]

GO DEEPER

- When have you been on pilgrimage—either a physical walk, a visit to a special place, or a journey that changed you? Recall the feelings this evoked in you.

- Just as paths unfold in front of us, so too do our own stories. Look back at your "way" up to this point. What turns have there been? What experiences made more sense later in life? How has Jesus accompanied you?

DELVE DEEPER

Fourteenth Sunday in Ordinary Time

GOSPEL: LUKE 10:1-12, 17-20

Peace to This House!

In today's gospel, Jesus appoints seventy-two disciples to go ahead of him to the towns he intends to visit. He recommends a specific greeting for them to use when entering a home, "Peace to this house!" The words set the tone for the visit, and we might compare it to the traditional Irish greeting, "God bless all here!" Jesus explains that, if a person of peace lives in the house, "your peace will go and rest on him," and the disciples will find a generous welcome in return. The peace that governs our home life extends to all, including strangers in need.

It is significant that peace is the first blessing that Jesus advises his followers to bring. As the COVID-19 pandemic gave rise to repeated lockdowns, one of the shocking statistics that emerged told of the increase in domestic violence. This particularly affected women who had no respite in their homes from abusive partners, and it gave rise to a surge in calls for help being reported by charities that support women and children.

Violence or abuse has no place in our homes or in our relationships. Jesus calls us to be people of peace in all our dealings with others. Peace does not mean constant harmony or the absence of disagreements. But how we treat our families and the people we live with should be governed by a peace that comes from a deep respect for the other and a willingness to listen, to understand, and to help. The peace we nurture at home will extend to all we meet. In Jesus' vision, it goes hand in hand with hospitality.

> *We find it so difficult to accept the revelation that it is God's delight to be worshipped in the way we touch and look at each other, in the way we listen and talk to each other, in the way we forgive and promise to start all over again.*
>
> ◆ DANIEL O'LEARY [54]

GO DEEPER

- Before we receive Eucharist, we pray for peace and unity in the community. Next time you enter a household, silently say the words, "Peace to this house!" and include all who are gathered in the blessing.

- Is there someone in your life with whom you are not at peace? How might you take steps to heal that relationship? In prayer, send peace to this person or into that situation.

Fifteenth Sunday in Ordinary Time

GOSPEL: LUKE 10:25-37

A Famous Parable

In today's gospel, we read of a lawyer who is trying to trick Jesus by asking him, "Who is my neighbor?" Jesus' response is the parable of the good Samaritan, where he tells the story of a man who is left half dead by robbers on his way from Jerusalem to Jericho. Our attention is drawn to the three characters who come upon the scene. The priest, the Levite, and the Samaritan all "see" the injured man, but the first two decide to "pass by." Those listening to this parable may well have found themselves sympathizing with the priest and the Levite, since there were purity laws preventing them from coming into contact with blood or a dead body. However, they are also bound by a responsibility to save the man's life, which should override any other concern they may have. It is most likely that the priest and the Levite were carrying oil and wine with them to make sacrifices in the Temple. If so, they could have been used to clean the wounds of the injured man, since oil and wine were vital parts of a first-century first-aid kit. Implicit here is a question about how we truly worship God.

So which of the three is truly a neighbor to this man? Jesus reveals the hero of this parable to be the third, a Samaritan. This would have sparked outrage among those listening, since Jews and Samaritans were enemies. Yet it is the Samaritan—the enemy—who is moved with pity, binds the man's wounds, pours oil on them, and takes him to an inn. He gives money to pay for his stay, but more important, he gives his time, caring for the man's immediate and long-term needs.

The emphasis in this parable is on compassion and action. Jesus points to a God who is not concerned with the boundaries we create, but who is on the streets with the injured, offering healing and mercy. The lawyer's question is about what limits are to be placed on neighborly love. Jesus tells us that there are no limits in God's eyes. Holiness is not in separating oneself from the injured, but in coming close to those in need.

> *Our prayer, our worship, our fasting are of little value to God if we have ignored those of God's children who suffer on the margins of our societies. We are Christians who follow the message of Jesus, not because we say "Lord, Lord"...it is in our compassion that we imitate God who is compassion.*
>
> ♦ PETER MCVERRY, SJ [55]

GO DEEPER

- Who are those left "half dead" in our society today? How can we be neighbors to them?

- We are so familiar with the phrase "good Samaritan" that this parable has almost lost its punch. The Samaritan was considered an enemy in Jesus' time. How might this story be told today? When has an "enemy" helped you?

Sixteenth Sunday in Ordinary Time

GOSPEL: LUKE 10:38–42

Martha and Mary

Jesus visits the home of Mary and Martha in today's gospel. It may be that Jesus has arrived unexpectedly with some of his followers, which would explain why Martha is so stressed. The account of this visit occurs in Luke's gospel immediately after the parable of the good Samaritan, so one would expect that Martha would be praised for serving the needs of her visitors. Instead, Jesus invites Martha to be nourished in a different way.

For such a short passage, this text has created much discussion among biblical scholars over the years. Mary is presented in this gospel as a disciple, sitting at Jesus' feet, learning from her Teacher. Throughout his gospel, Luke places a special emphasis on the wider circle of Jesus' disciples, and here he uses a specific word (*diakonia*) to refer to the "many tasks" that Martha was concerned about. This word is used elsewhere in Luke and Acts to refer to ministry and service in the early Church community. It is from this word that we get the word "deacon," and we know that there were female deacons in the early Church communities (Rom 16:1; 1 Tim 3:8–12; see also Gal 3:27–28).

However we interpret the roles of Mary and Martha in the Jesus community, this is a beautiful passage about the importance of being nourished by Jesus for ministry in all its forms. There is a time for action, but constant frantic activity is neither healthy nor sustainable. When we are so bogged down in the craziness around us, Jesus is clear about the way forward. First, sit and listen to him; then we may be better prepared for the challenges that we face.

> *Jesus stands out from his contemporaries like a glorious ray of sunshine in his respect for and his ability to relate to women.... This leveling of human and social injustice is at the heart of the message of Jesus, and has over the centuries, called women to move beyond the patriarchal and hierarchical restrictions imposed on their lives.* ◆ MARY T. MALONE [56]

GO DEEPER

- When we are occupied with "many tasks" we can become drained, and if we ignore this for too long it can lead to burnout. How do you nourish yourself? Can you find more time to sit with Jesus?

- Look again at Jesus and Mary in today's gospel. Jesus transcended expectations about traditional women's roles. Where do we see a division of roles along gender lines played out in our Church today?

Seventeenth Sunday in Ordinary Time

GOSPEL: LUKE 11:1–13

Search and You Will Find

When it comes to prayer, it is often a question of finding what works for you. In recent times, many people have found prayer apps—such as "Pray as You Go"—extremely helpful, because they allow for guided prayer at different moments of the day, even if you are on a bus or walking to work. They encourage us to make our whole day into a prayer, and they can help us to connect with prayer even when we don't feel like praying or can't pray.

We've all been there, so we can sympathize with the disciples' request of Jesus in today's gospel, "Lord, teach us to pray." It may surprise us to hear that Jesus gives them a very direct response—actual words in a formula to be recited. In Jesus' time there were many rabbis—teachers—who had certain prayers they expected their followers to say, almost as a mark of identity for their group. The Lord's Prayer is the prayer of the Jesus community, and it's our prayer too. It is perhaps the first prayer we learn as children and, in a moment of crisis, it is often the go-to prayer when all other words fail us.

After the Lord's Prayer, Jesus tells a story about a man whose friend goes to him at midnight requesting bread for an unexpected guest. It might appear to be a confusing story, but the parable teaches us to keep the needs of others in mind when we pray. In the early Church, and still today, this is seen as the work of the people of God. So, the first call is to prayer, and then to open that prayer out to the world.

> *Prayer brings us back to solid ground...bends our attention*
> *away from ourselves back toward God, and then to those who*
> *have been entrusted to our love and practical care: family,*
> *friends, community, and especially those who lack the blessings*
> *we have been given so abundantly.* ◆ COLUMBA STEWART [57]

GO DEEPER

- Can you recall who taught you your first prayers? Prayer can be as simple as a conversation with Jesus about your day. We also bring to mind those less fortunate than ourselves and those we find hard to forgive. Keep this in mind this week as you pray.

- Growth on the spiritual path involves making our whole day a prayer by offering our work, our words, and actions to God. Try to remain in this awareness this week.

Eighteenth Sunday in Ordinary Time

GOSPEL: LUKE 12:13-21

Profit and Loss

There is an Irish phrase that says, "You never see a trailer being pulled after a hearse." This would be a good way to sum up today's parable. Jesus tells us about a rich man with a storage problem. He places his sense of security in accumulating more and more wealth, so much so that he needs to build bigger barns to store his grain. For all his wealth, he does not realize his life is about to end. Nothing is more destructive to the human spirit than a preoccupation with accumulating more and more wealth, in whatever form it takes. It is usually driven by insecurity and a lack of peace. We try to constantly fill the gap in our lives that can only be filled by God.

A preoccupation with storing up stuff also affects our relationships with the world, especially with the poor. We cannot be in communion with our human family if we are hoarding resources while others are in need. In many countries people suffer as they struggle to maintain basic food security, while others live in extravagant luxury. It is shocking to read that, globally, one-third of all food is wasted. It is a lie to say that we do not have enough for everyone. As Mahatma Gandhi famously said, "The world has enough for everyone's need, but not enough for everyone's greed."

Humanity is at a crossroads where our habits of consumption are concerned. We now know that the Earth and her ecosystems are at the breaking point because of the continued exploitation of the resources necessary to feed our consumption habits. According to scientists, we would need three planet Earths to maintain our current rates of production. The parable today is urging us to focus on what is truly important.

> *When nature is viewed solely as a source of profit and gain, this has serious consequences for society. This...has engendered immense inequality, injustice and acts of violence against the majority of humanity....Completely at odds with this model are the ideals of harmony, justice, fraternity and peace as proposed by Jesus.* ◆ POPE FRANCIS [58]

GO DEEPER

- We start with ourselves. Can you declutter your life? Look around your home this week and see what could be donated to a charity shop.

- Over-consumption is extremely destructive and often occurs to fill a gap within ourselves. Can you be more aware when shopping in the coming weeks of what you really need?

Nineteenth Sunday in Ordinary Time

GOSPEL: LUKE 12:32–48

Dressed for Action

Jesus regularly emphasizes the importance of waiting. The sort of waiting he has in mind, however, does not mean sitting around until something happens—it means "active waiting," and there is an art to it. In today's parable, Jesus emphasizes the importance of being "dressed for action with "lamps lit," like servants waiting for their master to return from a wedding feast. The ideal servants are industrious, looking after others as they wait to welcome their master, while the less worthy servants, forgetting their purpose, are distracted by trivial things and engage in mistreating others.

The early Christians must have eagerly listened to this parable, as they were expecting Jesus to return very soon and were eager to be ready. What can it say to us today? In this digital age, we have endless options for entertainment. At the touch of a screen, we can fill our minds with news, social events, videos, and games; our smart technologies have literally become an extension of our arms. We can seldom claim to be bored or idle. But are we living present, vigilant lives? Are we giving our full care and attention to those we live with and their needs? Are we awake to God's presence in the vibrancy of life around us, in all of creation?

Jesus finishes his parable with a warning for those who know what is required "but did not prepare." This may resonate with us. We tend to postpone serious reflection about our life and habits, thinking we have plenty of time. We distract ourselves and avoid really living in the fullness of life with our lamps lit and our minds always tuned to God.

> *It's a terrible thing, I think, in life to wait until you're ready. I have this feeling now that actually no one is ever ready to do anything. There is almost no such thing as ready. There is only now. And you may as well do it now....Generally speaking, now is as good a time as any.* ◆ HUGH LAURIE [59]

GO DEEPER

- Jesus starts this parable by instructing the disciples to sell their possessions and give alms; in other words, to live simply and share generously. This is one way we can be "dressed for action." How can you embrace this lifestyle?

- Look back over the past week. Where was God present for you? Ask for the grace to be more alert to God's presence in the coming week.

Twentieth Sunday in Ordinary Time

GOSPEL: LUKE 12:49–53

Peace on Earth?

It is only a few weeks since we heard Jesus advising his disciples to greet people with the words, "Peace to this house!" We associate Jesus with peace rather than division. When he greets the disciples after the resurrection, his first words are "Peace be with you." Yet here he is talking about division, even within households and families.

At the time Luke was writing his gospel, the early Christian community was experiencing division, and many households were torn apart over what to believe. It was Jesus' desire that the flame of his Good News would burn brightly—"I came to bring fire to the earth"—but not everyone was ready for his radical vision, and division was the natural and painful consequence. We still live in a divided world when it comes to Jesus' message. Different factions in the Church argue and swipe at each other, often in very unchristian ways, lacking genuine respect or dialogue. Parents and grandparents can be hurt when younger family members drift away from the faith or have a different way of practicing it. Some people walk away because they feel unwelcome or betrayed by the Church.

A certain amount of conflict is unavoidable as we navigate our changing faith landscape, but we do have a choice. Do we allow anger and hurt to shape our interactions, or do we try to listen and to heal, as Jesus did in his encounters with others? None of us has all the answers, but we seek and move forward together hoping that a better world is ahead, and that Jesus is guiding us ever closer to the peace he promised.

> *The peace promised by God does not come from accepting the world as it is....The Christian community was established by Jesus in order to show a broken world how to live as the new creation which Jesus promised for the future. The Christian community, by the way we live, love, care and share with each other, is called to say "No" to our world as it is, to say "Yes" to the world as it should be.* ◆ PETER MCVERRY, SJ [60]

GO DEEPER

- This is a disturbing gospel. Take some time to read it again and sit with Jesus in this moment as he contemplates the divisions in our world.

- Reflect on your own family relationships. Ask Jesus to come into any areas of hurt or conflict you can identify, and to guide you as you navigate them.

Solemnity of the Assumption

GOSPEL: LUKE 1:39–56

Lifting Up

We sometimes think of Mary simply as a meek character, timidly accepting God's challenging plan for her. In today's gospel we see another side of her and find that she is far from timid. The entire exchange between Mary and Elizabeth is filled with giddy joy. When Elizabeth hears Mary's greeting, she is filled with the Holy Spirit and calls Mary "blessed" as she cries out with delight. Mary responds with a spontaneous hymn, "My soul magnifies the Lord, and my spirit rejoices in God my Savior." Hope fills the house as Elizabeth recognizes who is paying her a visit—her relative Mary, yes, but someone who is so much more!

In the words of that powerful hymn, the Magnificat, Mary reveals a God who turns things upside down, who is on the side of the poor and oppressed as opposed to the rich and powerful. This God who "lifts up the lowly" is the God who will be revealed in Jesus. So Mary's words act as a manifesto for her unborn baby, announcing the dream of God for the world.

Today, with Mary, we think of the painful circumstances of those who are downtrodden. We remember in particular the many women oppressed by violence and inequality, and those who are trafficked or exploited. Pope Francis has highlighted the plight of women who "await the day in which they will finally feel they are held by hands which do not humiliate them, but which lift them tenderly and lead them on the path of life." [61] In these early days of Mary's extraordinary journey, she is setting the agenda for the ministry of Jesus, who came to "bring good news to the poor...to proclaim release to the captives...to let the oppressed go free" (Lk 4:18–19).

> *These words are a rebel's anthem. Mary, through the goodness and grace of God, is saying yes to the Kingdom and no to the Empire. She is rejoicing in God her savior who flips the world upside down and puts all things to right.* ◆ BRENT NEELY [62]

GO DEEPER

- When Mary prayed the Magnificat, she knew she was pregnant with Jesus. Pray the words with her: experience her joy, her sense that something great was happening, the hope and promise that she carried within her.

- From the very beginning of Jesus' story, the focus was on "lifting up" those who are poor and oppressed. Our mission as his followers is to lift up those who suffer. How can we live the Magnificat today?

GOSPEL: LUKE 13:22-30

Strive to Enter through the Narrow Door

In today's gospel, as Jesus continues on his Way, he is asked, "Will only a few be saved?" Many in the crowd, and in the early Christian communities, would have assumed they were "saved" because they were contemporaries of Jesus or because of their social status. Jesus' response is the parable of the narrow door, which is not about who will be saved, or how many; it is about walking a particular path.

Through his ministry, Jesus has shown us what the Kingdom of God is like. This dream of God motivated all that Jesus said and did (Lk 4:18–21). We are told that this Kingdom is within us, or in our midst (Lk 17:21), to be achieved in our time and space. This Kingdom will therefore require an inner transformation. It is interesting that Jesus uses the image of a narrow door. Doors are means of connecting one place with another. On our spiritual journeys, we should feel nourished and be shown how to move forward, not remain in a dead place.

This parable warns against complacency, encouraging us to go deeper. It demands that we strive continuously to grow in our awareness, discovering new depths about ourselves and our humanity. This Way requires effort and inner freedom. There are many obstacles and distractions that can prevent us from progressing on this path, which is why the Way is narrow and crowded. Yet, it is not an impossible task.

To ask "who will be saved?" misses the point completely. Jesus says people will be welcomed from "east and west, from north and south." This path is available to all. God's dream is not only for a select few.

[Jesus] says, "The Kingdom of Heaven is within you" (that is, here) and "at hand" (that is, now). It's not later, but lighter— some more subtle quality or dimension of experience accessible to you right in the moment. You don't die into it; you awaken into it. ◆ CYNTHIA BOURGEAULT [63]

GO DEEPER

- Reflect this week on your spiritual life. Are you bored? Have things become stale? Sometimes we need guidance from a friend or spiritual companion, or we might make a retreat. Think about what you can do to cultivate a deeper awareness.

- The door is "narrow." What obstacles are there in your own path that prevent you from "striving" for inner transformation?

Twenty-Second Sunday in Ordinary Time

GOSPEL: LUKE 14:1, 7-14

All Are Invited to the Banquet.

In Luke's gospel, a key part of Jesus' ministry is table fellowship. More than in any of the other gospels, Luke shows Jesus eating and drinking at table. Today he is at the house of a Pharisee for a Sabbath meal, while the other guests watch him closely. Jesus, noticing how the guests are vying with each other for the seats of honor, tells a parable. At first glance, this story might seem to be suggesting that we deceive others with a false humility, but remember parables always encourage us to think more deeply. They are designed to stay with us for rumination. And so, it is good to pay attention to the questions that arise.

Jesus frequently used the image of a great banquet to explain God's vision for our world. The feast that is described here emphasizes hospitality to strangers, and not just any strangers. Jesus speaks of a preferential option for the poor, the crippled, the lame, and the blind. They are outsiders, because of their circumstances, and also because they are considered to be ritually unclean. This parable urges us to be open to real people and their very real situations, breaking down societal barriers to embrace real relationships. This is where one encounters the energy of the Kingdom on earth.

Jesus made it clear that his mission was to release people from whatever it was that made them feel estranged from God (Lk 4:18–21). We are called to partake in this mission, welcoming those considered to be on the outside without any hope of reward for ourselves. The feast in today's gospel is a great celebration of inclusivity and unity. It emphasizes once more the reversal Jesus talks about, where the "highest" take the low seats and the world is turned upside down for the better. There is no shortage of situations in our world in need of this type of shake-up. Our task is to help bring it about.

> *Another world is not only possible; she is on her way....On a quiet day, if I listen very carefully, I can hear her breathing.*
> ◆ ARUNDHATI ROY [64]

GO DEEPER

- What situations in your local community need to be turned upside down, so that those considered least are given preferential treatment? Bring these to prayer. What are you being called to?

- Being considered "ritually unclean" is a practice that continues today. In our Church people are excluded from the Table because of their sexuality or their personal situations. How can we embrace Jesus' inclusivity in our local Church communities?

⤞ 7.1 ⤝

The Season of Creation

Introduction to the Season of Creation

(1 SEPTEMBER — 4 OCTOBER)

Within Ordinary Time, the Season of Creation gives us an opportunity to come together to renew our relationship with God's creation. It runs from the World Day of Prayer for Creation on 1 September to the Feast of St. Francis of Assisi on 4 October. It has its origins in the Orthodox Church, which in 1989 proclaimed 1 September as a day of prayer for creation. Subsequently, the World Council of Churches extended the celebration until 4 October. Many Christians around the world embraced this idea, and in 2015 Pope Francis officially declared 1 September the World Day of Prayer for Creation in the Catholic calendar. This means that the world's 2.2 billion Christians now celebrate the Season of Creation as an ecumenical occasion worldwide.

In 2015 Pope Francis published his ground-breaking encyclical on the environment, *Laudato Si'*. In it he calls on all people of the world to enter into dialogue about what is happening to our planet, urging us to listen to both the cry of the earth and the cry of the poor. He invites us to "become painfully aware" of the extent of this crisis, and to engage in the conversion that is needed to protect our common home. In light of the urgent ecological crisis our world is facing and the addition of the Season of Creation to our liturgical calendar, the reflections for the next five Sundays will focus on this theme, as well as paying attention to the gospel of the day.

All Christians are invited to embrace this season wholeheartedly, through deep reflection, through living more sustainably, through raising our voices in the public sphere, and in a special way through our liturgies. We are invited to think more deeply about what is happening at present to the earth, to recognize the environmental destruction that now threatens our world, and to accept the call to "eco-conversion."

> *I wish to address every person living on this planet....I urgently appeal for a new dialogue about how we are shaping the future of our planet. We need a conversation which includes everyone, since the environmental challenge we are undergoing, and its human roots, concern and affect us all.*
>
> ◆ POPE FRANCIS [65]

SEASON OF CREATION 1 » GOSPEL: LUKE 14:25–33

The Cost of Discipleship

Today's gospel is troubling. Does Jesus really expect us to hate our families, friends, and even ourselves in order to be his followers? The call to "hate" our family is not to be taken literally but is a call for us to break free from any habit or relationship holding us back. If you reflect back on a time when you gained a significant new insight, you may find that it involved letting go of something you were attached to. Attachments can cause all sorts of suffering in our lives; moving on from what we find comfortable can be painful, but that is how we grow.

In *Laudato Si'*, Pope Francis calls each of us to become "painfully aware" of what is happening to our world. We know now that the past two hundred years of "development" have caused widespread destruction of our planet, altering the very fabric of our ecosystems. We want to maintain that pattern as if infinite economic growth could continue indefinitely, but this is simply not possible on a planet with finite resources. Levels of consumption by humans are out of control. We have not considered the full cost of building the "tower" Jesus talks about in today's gospel.

The Season of Creation is a time to reconnect with the beauty of God's creation so that we can set out on more sustainable paths. This involves breaking away from systems on which we are dependent and embracing a gentler way of walking on this earth. It requires a drastic change of heart so that we can set out on new paths as a global community.

The ecological crisis is also a summons to profound interior conversion...whereby the effects of our encounter with Jesus Christ become evident in our relationship with the world around us. Living our vocation to be protectors of God's handiwork is essential to a life of virtue; it is not an optional or a secondary aspect of our Christian experience.

◆ POPE FRANCIS [66]

GO DEEPER

- During this Season of Creation you might decide to read *Laudato Si'* and invite some people to join you. Ask your parish pastoral council to include a quote per week in their parish newsletter. Reflect on other ways of sharing this wisdom with the wider community.

- Encourage your family to make one small change this week, such as using public transport, walking/cycling when possible, and ensuring that all waste is correctly recycled or composted. We start with ourselves.

Twenty-Fourth Sunday in Ordinary Time

SEASON OF CREATION 2 » GOSPEL: LUKE 15:1–32 [67]

Coming to Our Senses

In the parables about the lost sheep and the lost coin, we hear how God celebrates when those who stray are returned to the community. In the third parable about the lost son, we hear that the younger brother eventually "came to himself" or came to his senses as we might say. By entering into a greater awareness, he realized that he had made wrong choices and had a change of heart. We might focus today on how we too must come to our senses in our lives, especially during this Season of Creation.

We lament the destruction of God's creation and the loss of biodiversity that is due to human activity. God's creatures are disappearing from the Earth at a rate we can scarcely comprehend. In 2020 the Living Planet Report concluded that 68% of wildlife had disappeared in the period from 1970 to 2016. [68] We are living through the sixth mass extinction of life in our planet's history, and this one is being driven by human over-consumption. For example, by destroying our great rainforests we destroy not only trees but also the habitats of birds, insects, mammals, and plants that will never be seen again. Pope Francis invites us to "feel the desertification of the soil almost as a physical ailment and the extinction of a species as a painful disfigurement" (*Laudato Si'* §89). We are part of, and dependent on, complex and delicate ecosystems that make up the web of life. This web is now unravelling, and we know we humans cannot be healthy on a planet that is not itself healthy.

The enormity of this crisis threatens to overwhelm us. Yet hope is found in action. Like the lost son in today's gospel, we are capable of coming to our senses, choosing again what is good, and making a new start. As with all significant change, this begins at the grassroots—with you and me.

> *Because all creatures are connected, each must be cherished with love and respect, for all of us as living creatures are dependent on one another.* • POPE FRANCIS [69]

GO DEEPER

- As local Church communities, we can lead by example. We can rewild our church grounds by planting native trees and create wildflower areas for pollinators. We can invite local eco-groups to learn from them. What are you being called to do?

- Single-use plastics cause untold damage to our fragile ecosystems, especially our rivers and oceans. Can you remove single-use plastics from your life? Buy a reusable water bottle and reusable coffee cup. Say no to plastic straws and food wrapping.

Twenty-Fifth Sunday in Ordinary Time

SEASON OF CREATION 3 » GOSPEL: LUKE 16:1-13

Kingdom Economics

If you think that all the parables of Jesus are pleasant stories about people of integrity, then today's gospel might make you think again. In this story, a manager has been given his notice by his CEO and decides, while he still can, to even up the tables for those who are struggling to pay their debts to the company. He uses the power he still has to change the future for these debtors—and for himself. He is happy to make better arrangements for the debtors. The manager is free-spirited, a bit of a scoundrel, yes, but Jesus liked scoundrels, once their efforts were put to good use. The only value the money really has is in the way it is used. He is squandering money, but he is not squandering opportunities.

When it comes to the reality of our climate crisis, change is urgently needed at political levels. The science is clear: our world is warming because of human activity, giving rise to drought, famine, devastating wildfires, extreme weather events, a rise in sea levels, and the displacement of millions of people. On our current trajectory, many parts of our world will be uninhabitable in the decades to come.

Climate change is one of the biggest challenges facing our world today, and it has grave implications for many aspects of our lives: environmental, social, economic, and political. We know that just a hundred fossil fuel companies are responsible for seventy percent of the carbon emissions that drive this crisis. These corporations care little for future generations. Young people are standing up to such systems, however, calling them to account, engaging in political action, and challenging all of us to raise our voices for our common home. They tell us that change is coming whether we like it or not. [70] Today's parable invites us, like the manager, to "holy mischief." [71]

> *What kind of world do we want to leave to those who come after us, to children who are now growing up?...We may well be leaving to coming generations debris, desolation and filth.*
> ◆ POPE FRANCIS [72]

GO DEEPER

- Local faith communities can create awareness and take action on the climate crisis by writing to politicians, supporting youth climate movements, listening to the experiences and concerns of young people, and inviting them to speak at events. What "holy mischief" are you being called to?

- Many dioceses and parishes have started effective initiatives encouraging Christian communities to become eco-parishes, shining as examples of what is possible in order to address this crisis. Why not consider getting involved?

Twenty-Sixth Sunday in Ordinary Time

SEASON OF CREATION 4 » GOSPEL: LUKE 16:19–31

A Great Reversal

In Luke's gospel, there is an emphasis on *seeing* the poor and the oppressed. The rich man in today's gospel does not "see" Lazarus, and even in the afterlife he is still blinded and unwilling to change. He wants Lazarus to be sent to his brothers to warn them, for they too do not really *see*. Their vision has been blinded by wealth, and they do not *see* the reality of the poor who are at their gates. God's economic plan means striving for a world where the poor man Lazarus can sit down at the same table as the rich man, and where we listen to the cry of the poor.

Joanna Sustento is from Tacloban City in the Philippines. In the storm surge of Typhoon Hayan on 8 November 2013, she lost her parents, her brother, her sister-in-law, and her three-year-old nephew Tarin. Joanna was the only person to survive from her household that night. This was the largest typhoon ever to make landfall in recorded history. Ten thousand people perished in two hours, and fourteen million were displaced. The strength of Typhoon Haiyan is attributed by scientists to climate change.

It is an injustice that those who have done the least to cause this problem are on the front lines of the crisis. When we hear the scientific data, we easily become detached. When we hear real stories, however, and see the devastation and grief of families, we can be moved by compassion to act. We are at a crossroads as a global community: we have the solutions to move forward into a more sustainable future for all, but we are in danger of failing for lack of political will. May today's gospel truly remind us to *see* the realities of this ecological crisis so that we can act for the protection of all life on earth.

> *Time is running out....We do not have the luxury of waiting for others to step forward, or of prioritizing short-term economic benefits. The climate crisis requires our decisive action, here and now and the Church is fully committed to playing her part.*
>
> ◆ POPE FRANCIS [73]

GO DEEPER

- Sharing the stories of people who are on the front lines of the environmental crisis is so important. How can your community hear these voices more clearly?

- In May 2021 Pope Francis announced the *Laudato Si'* Goals, a seven-year plan toward a more sustainable world. Can your school, parish, diocese, or family get involved? Find out more this week about this call to action. [74]

Twenty-Seventh Sunday in Ordinary Time

SEASON OF CREATION 5 » GOSPEL: LUKE 17:5–10

The Gaze of Jesus

In today's gospel we hear Jesus speaking about mustard seeds, mulberry trees, sheep, fields, the sea, and ploughs. Jesus spent most of his time in the midst of nature. He went to quiet places to pray; his entire ministry involved walking from place to place; he preached on mountaintops and in boats on the sea; some of his followers were fishermen. The son of a carpenter, Jesus no doubt "worked with his hands, in daily contact with the matter created by God, to which he gave form by his craftsmanship" (*Laudato Si'* §99).

The roots of the environmental crisis our world faces are deeply spiritual, for we have become detached from the beauty of the natural world. This affects us deeply, even if we are not aware of it. *Laudato Si'* reminds us that we were never meant to be surrounded by asphalt, metal, cement, and glass, and it invites us to rekindle a childlike sense of awe and wonder at nature. So, if we are looking for a place to begin, we begin here. We must reconnect with nature, for we will only protect what we love. Let us reawaken ourselves to the fact that "the entire material universe speaks of God's love, his boundless affection for us. Soil, water, mountains: everything is, as it were, a caress of God" (*Laudato Si'* §84).

The realities of the ecological crisis can be overwhelming, but Jesus reminds us today to strive for that which seems impossible. As we draw near to the end of this Season of Creation, let it be a springboard into contemplation and action in our relationship with God's creation. Let us live *Laudato Si'*. Truly, much can be done!

> *God has written a precious book, whose letters are the multitude of created things. From panoramic vistas to the tiniest living form, nature is a constant source of wonder and awe....There is a divine manifestation in the blaze of the sun and the fall of night.* • POPE FRANCIS [75]

GO DEEPER

- Spend time in the midst of nature this week, with increased awareness. What do you see, smell, touch, hear, or even taste? Feel the ground beneath your feet, the wind in your face, the rain and the sun. All of it a "caress of God." [76]

- Where is your favorite place in nature? Bring it to mind. How do you feel when you are in that place? Maybe you could write about it. Perhaps you can spend more time there, "standing awestruck before a mountain..." (*Laudato Si'* §234).

Feast of St. Francis of Assisi

SEASON OF CREATION 6 » GOSPEL: MATTHEW 11:25-30

Everything Is Connected

The feast of St. Francis of Assisi is celebrated each year on 4 October. It marks the end of the Season of Creation; it invites us to celebrate the patron saint of ecology and to learn from him. St. Francis was intimately connected with nature. His famous prayer, the "Canticle of the Sun," refers to "Brother Sun, Sister Moon, Brother Wind, Sister Water." [77] St. Francis was a mystic who, "faithful to Scripture, invites us to see nature as a magnificent book in which God speaks to us and grants us a glimpse of his infinite beauty and goodness" (*Laudato Si'* §12).

Aware of just how deeply interconnected everything is, St. Francis had a deep grasp of what we today call integral ecology. Just as Jesus spent much time in nature, contemplating the sparrows (Lk 12:6) and the tiniest of seeds (Lk 17:5), so St. Francis also lived in full harmony with creation. St. Francis showed us that care for creation is inseparable from concern for each other, justice for the poor, and our own interior peace. Seeing that everything is connected, and living out this vision joyfully and with an open heart, St. Francis was—and is—deeply loved. He takes us to the heart of what it is to be human and invites us to a profound interior conversion: "Just as happens when we fall in love with someone, whenever St. Francis would gaze at the sun, the moon or the smallest of animals, he burst into song, drawing all other creatures into his praise" (*Laudato Si'* §11).

We are called into this awareness so that we repair our broken relationship with the natural world and with each other. We are called to turn away from destruction and, feeling intimately connected to all that exists, care more deeply for our common home.

> *The risen One is mysteriously holding [creatures] to himself and directing them towards fullness as their end. The very flowers of the field and the birds which his human eyes contemplated and admired are now imbued with his radiant presence.*
>
> ♦ POPE FRANCIS [78]

GO DEEPER

- To mark the feast of St. Francis, many parishes host a blessing of animals. Pets are such an important part of our lives. Today is an opportunity to give thanks to God for pets and celebrate the gift of companionship they offer us. It's an opportunity for us to remember pets that have died.

- Look back on the Season of Creation and gather the fruits. What was your experience? What new insights have you gained? What new invitations are calling to you?

Twenty-Eighth Sunday in Ordinary Time

GOSPEL: LUKE 17:11–19

Thank You!

What a difference an attitude of gratitude makes! In today's gospel, the life of the man who turns back to thank Jesus is utterly transformed. The other nine receive the same gift of healing, but they do not acknowledge the gift or the giver. In thanking Jesus, the Samaritan man enters into a relationship with him; he becomes a disciple.

During the early days of the COVID-19 pandemic, there was an outpouring of gratitude for healthcare workers. People stood outside their homes to clap for the nurses, doctors, and first responders who were putting their lives on the line. There were campaigns for better pay and conditions for them and appeals to the public to play their part in keeping these heroes safe. But over time the clapping stopped, and the media spotlight moved on, though of course the selfless work continued.

Gratitude makes us aware that we are part of something bigger than ourselves by being connected to others and the world. Pope Francis has spoken of the importance of saying "thank you" in family life, and he suggests that we should give thanks before and after meals: "That moment of blessing, however brief, reminds us of our dependence on God for life; it strengthens our feeling of gratitude for the gifts of creation; it acknowledges those who by their labour provide us with these goods; and it reaffirms our solidarity with those in greatest need." [79]

We slip easily into the habit of turning to prayer only when we need something. But what about after the storm has passed? Jesus asks the question, "The other nine, where are they?" Perhaps they simply got on with their lives and, over time, let the memory fade. All ten were healed, yet, because of his gratitude, one man had a fuller experience, and his life was all the richer.

> *Gratitude unlocks the fullness of life. It turns what we have into enough, and more. It turns denial into acceptance, chaos to order, confusion to clarity. It can turn a meal into a feast, a house into a home, a stranger into a friend.*
> ◆ MELODY BEATTIE [80]

GO DEEPER

- Gratitude is an important part of faith. Make a list of all the blessings you are grateful for in your life. Write a letter to someone expressing gratitude for all they mean to you.

- Take a few moments to remember all those who care for the sick, whether at home or in healthcare settings. Give thanks for all they do, and ask God to bless them in their work.

Twenty-Ninth Sunday in Ordinary Time

GOSPEL: LUKE 18:1–8

Crying Out

The judge in the parable we hear about today is hardly a role model. He delivers justice to the widow, not because he cares, but because he wants to get rid of her. He is painted in contrast with God, who is full of compassion, particularly for those most in need. When we cry out, God hears us. On the surface, the parable seems to be about the need to persevere in prayer, but like all of Jesus' parables, it has layers of meaning. At the time of Jesus, many widows were left without resources following the death of their husbands. Jewish listeners would have been aware that the Hebrew Scriptures called for the protection of widows as well as the poor and foreigners, so the woman in today's parable represents all these vulnerable groups.

Today, vulnerable people continue to cry out for justice, and their cries often fall on deaf ears. As a society, are we like the unjust judge, ignoring them and hoping they will go away or that someone else will deal with them? Do we offer a half-hearted response, just to soothe our conscience? Or is our response rooted in a real sense of compassion and justice?

There is another sting in the tail of today's gospel. Almost as an afterthought, Jesus poses a challenge, "But when the Son of Man comes, will he find any faith on earth?" The real question is not whether our prayer can move God, but rather, Jesus suggests, if our prayer can move us. Does our faith spur us into action? The widow refused to stop fighting until justice was granted. We cannot sit back and expect our prayers to be answered without effort on our part. Our prayer life goes hand in hand with our willingness to fight for what is right.

> *We need to acknowledge that we are constantly tempted to ignore others, especially the weak. Let us admit that, for all the progress we have made, we are still "illiterate" when it comes to accompanying, caring for and supporting the most frail and vulnerable members of our developed societies. We have become accustomed to looking the other way, passing by, ignoring situations until they affect us directly.* • POPE FRANCIS [81]

- Who are the vulnerable people today who are crying out for justice? How do our political and social systems respond to them? How do I respond?

- We are called to help bring about God's vision for this world. Bring these situations of injustice to prayer. How are you being called to act?

Thirtieth Sunday in Ordinary Time

GOSPEL: LUKE 18:9-14

Being Right with God

In the parable in today's gospel, we are invited to place ourselves in the shoes of two characters who represent extreme ways of being in the world. The Pharisee's superior attitude immediately jumps out. He knows nothing of the efforts of the man praying behind him. Yet he dismisses him, and with him all humankind, as "thieves, rogues, adulterers." As a religious leader, he believes he has the moral high ground because he fasts and pays tithes, the outward shows of virtue.

The tax collector, on the other hand, simply asks God for help. He is aware of his sinfulness, but open to hope and change. As Jesus interprets the parable for his audience of "righteous" people, he perhaps shocks them by telling them that the tax collector is the one who is right with God. In Luke's gospel, expectations are often subverted, as summarized in the closing words of this parable, "For all who exalt themselves will be humbled, but all who humble themselves will be exalted." This is a key teaching of Jesus repeated several times in Luke's gospel (see Lk 1:52; 14:11).

While the characters are contrasted for effect, at different times we embody the characteristics of each of them. Like the Pharisee, we can rush to judgment, without even realizing we are doing so. We make presumptions about people based on their appearance, accent, background, or occupation. We place ourselves on the "inside," keeping others on the "outside." When we remember that all people have their struggles, we are a lot kinder. Both of the characters in today's parable would like to be right with God, but they have a different understanding of what that relationship entails. When we come into greater awareness, God's grace is there.

> *Then and now there are those for whom the good news is that there are insiders and outsiders and that we get to be on the inside. But to others, the good news is that there no longer are outsiders.* • NADIA BOLZ WEBER [82]

GO DEEPER

- The greatest insights in life can come from unexpected sources. Is there someone at home, school, or work whom you could spend time getting to know, perhaps a person you have judged or written off in the past?

- The prayer "God, be merciful to me" simply means "God, please heal me" or "God, please help me." Find a quiet time and repeat this phrase, sitting in the healing presence of God.

GOSPEL: LUKE 19:1-10

Salvation to This House

The story of Zacchaeus is one of the most familiar gospel stories, although it is only found in Luke. The vivid details easily resonate with us: the unpopular tax collector, too short to see Jesus, who climbs a tree to get a better view and then hears the startling words of Jesus, "Zacchaeus, hurry and come down; for I must stay at your house today." As he often does, Jesus goes against the social and religious expectations of his time. As a tax collector, Zacchaeus would have been considered unworthy, a sinner. While this already makes him an outsider, in this scene he is also literally on the outside of the crowd. He can't get a glimpse of Jesus, but in his determination to see him he climbs a tree.

Jesus sees Zacchaeus, however, and approaches him, creating shock among the onlookers. They grumble, unhappy to see Jesus reaching out to a "sinner." Then Jesus does something completely unexpected. He invites himself to Zacchaeus' home, where Jesus' pronouncement is equally unexpected, "Today, salvation has come to this house." This story ties in perfectly with the earlier parables of the Lost Coin, the Lost Sheep, and the Prodigal Son (Lk 15:1–32). There we are reminded of the rejoicing that takes place when what has been lost is found again. Jesus has come to save the lost.

In this story, it is significant that Jesus invites Zacchaeus into table fellowship, even before he decides to mend his ways and make restitution to those he has cheated. Zacchaeus welcomes Jesus to his house with open arms, and the experience of Jesus' love and acceptance transforms him. Jesus is waiting for our welcome today.

> *The question is not "How am I to find God?" but "How am I to let myself be found by [God]?"...God is looking into the distance for me, trying to find me, and longing to bring me home.*
>
> ◆ **HENRI J.M. NOUWEN** [83]

GO DEEPER

- Martin Luther King Jr. has said, "Hate cannot drive out hate; only love can do that." While the condemnation of the crowds kept Zacchaeus away from Jesus, the welcome and compassion of Jesus drew him near. Is there anyone you could reach out to in a similar way today?

- Zacchaeus was a seeker, drawn to Jesus. How can we as a Church reach out to those who are exploring and searching for deeper meaning in their lives? Do we welcome all seekers at the Table?

Solemnity of All Saints » 1 November

GOSPEL: MATTHEW 5:1-12

Called to Be Saints

"They'll have their reward in heaven": this comforting expression is often spoken in the days following a bereavement as a way of honoring someone who has lived a good life, who was honest, loving, kind, and worked hard for others. It gives voice to our deep sense that there is something beyond this life and that our loved one has passed into the welcoming presence of God and the community of saints.

As we celebrate the Solemnity of All Saints, our gospel reveals the original context of these words in the Beatitudes of Jesus.

However, when Jesus talks about the Kingdom of Heaven, as he does here, we are reminded that he is not only talking about the next life. The Beatitudes offer a vision for the here-and-now; they are a call to a world where justice and compassion prevail and there is no room for inequality. They have the power to turn the world as we know it upside down.

The saints we look up to embody many of the Beatitudes; they are like guides who have gone before us, holding a torch to show us the way. In our own lives, we have known people with these exceptional qualities, people who are gentle and kind, who live simply and peacefully, who fight for what is right, who work for peace, who weather pain and hurt with dignity. There are many saints who will never be canonized but who show us how to live well, teaching us about God with their lives.

We are all called to be saints and to nurture the attributes we read about in today's gospel. Today, let us take the opportunity to look beyond this life, to remember those who have gone before us, and to learn how we can live a life of fullness and holiness, embracing God's Kingdom here in the world.

> *Saints are those who wake up while in this world, instead of waiting for the next one.* ◆ RICHARD ROHR [84]

GO DEEPER

- Think of your favorite saints. What draws you to them, and how can you learn from their example? Pray to them for guidance.

- Today's gospel is taken from the Sermon on the Mount in Matthew's gospel. Reread the words of the Beatitudes. Perhaps reflect on one each day during the coming week. Where are they calling you?

Thirty-Second Sunday in Ordinary Time

GOSPEL: LUKE 20:27-38

Children of the Resurrection

Will I have a body in heaven? Will I look young or old? Will I recognize my family and friends? When we think about the afterlife, we can find ourselves preoccupied with questions like these. In today's gospel the Sadducees, who do not believe in the resurrection of the body, are setting a trap for Jesus with their clever technical question. They quote the Law of Moses, which prescribed that a man whose brother had died without children was obliged to marry his brother's widow. And then they pose a far-fetched scenario: whose wife will the woman be in heaven?

Jesus sidesteps the trap by making their question seem absurd. He affirms the reality of the life to come, but while we might think of heaven as an improved version of our earthly life, Jesus says the relationships and concerns of this life will be transformed in the next. Questions like the one posed by the Sadducees ignore the radical freshness of God's vision for us and for God's creation.

In this gospel, the talk of marrying reflects the customs of the time, when a woman could be "given" in marriage and was considered the property of her husband. Such things are in the realm of "worldly" concerns, as Jesus puts it, things that "belong to this age." He contrasts this with the coming age, where the "children of the resurrection" will belong to nobody but God. In this vision, divisions of class, status, or gender no longer exist. While the Sadducees impose their limited world-view on to God—as we humans tend to do—Jesus encourages us to live as "resurrection people" in the fullness of his mission to bring love, healing, and liberation to all (Lk 4:18).

> *The important question to ask is not "What do you believe?"*
> *but "What difference does it make that you believe?" Does the*
> *world come nearer to the dream of God because of what you*
> *believe?* • VERNA J. DOZIER [85]

GO DEEPER

- Bring to mind someone who has passed away, but who is very much alive because of the difference he or she made to others. Such people, who brought God's vision for the world to life, are "children of the resurrection."

- The resurrection is not just about life after death but life before death too: full, abundant life. Can we move from being "children of the world" to "children of the resurrection" in the here and now? What image does this conjure up for you?

Thirty-Third Sunday in Ordinary Time

GOSPEL: LUKE 21:5–19

Do Not Be Afraid.

As we approach the end of the Church year, we are also coming toward the end of Luke's gospel, and things have taken a dark turn. Jesus has arrived in Jerusalem, which means, as we know, that he is on course for a violent death. In an intense monologue, upsetting for his companions, he speaks of earthquakes and famines, persecution and death. While those around him are enjoying the magnificence of the Temple, Jesus tells them it will be totally destroyed. This is an unimaginable event, which they easily take to signify the end of the world. [86] Bleak words indeed.

This is Jesus' talk of the "end times," the kind that we still sometimes hear at times of crisis. There have always been disasters in the world, from wars and plagues to earthquakes and tsunamis, and many people have interpreted these things as signs of the end of the world. We face our own personal disasters, too, when we lose a loved one, when diagnosed with serious illness, when a relationship breaks down. At times like that we feel as if our world is ending. The recent pandemic comes to mind as an example. For many of us, it felt like the end of the world as we knew it, a never-ending endurance test.

In today's gospel, Jesus is preparing the disciples for what is about to happen to him, but in spite of the challenges ahead he offers encouragement: he will be with them. He promises "words and wisdom" when they are in difficulty. When we are facing a crisis, Jesus tells us not to be afraid. When we feel hopeless about the sadness and destruction in the world, he is there. We keep going, as best we can, in the messiness and brokenness of life. God's grace is with us and can change everything.

> *When we are young we think that we become great through our achievements. Life has taught us the truth of Jesus' words: it is by endurance that we win our lives.* • MICHEL DE VERTEUIL [87]

GO DEEPER

- We all have moments of darkness when things seem bleak. Think of a time when you experienced such hopelessness. What helped you to get through it? Where do your strength and comfort come from?

- When we hear news of natural disasters, pandemics, the destruction of great buildings, or the fall of empires, it can feel like "end times." But in the midst of the chaos there are always those who bring light and hope. When have you seen this to be true?

Solemnity of Christ the King

LAST SUNDAY IN ORDINARY TIME
GOSPEL: LUKE 23:35-43

A New Kind of Royalty

We have reached the last Sunday in the Church calendar. For the past year, we have been following the story of Jesus from the Gospel of Luke, and now, as he lies dying on the cross, questions are raised regarding his identity. People expected that the great messianic king would lead a rebellion and establish his kingdom on earth. Many of those Jesus encountered, including the religious and political elite, the crowds, and even at times his own disciples, expected Jesus to act like that sort of leader. The Jesus we meet on the cross is the exact opposite, which is why he is mocked. One of the criminals alongside him taunts him, "Are you not the Messiah? Save yourself and us!" A true king would surely be able to avoid humiliation and death, he thinks. Jesus is a different sort of king, however, and at this moment the other criminal recognizes this. In turn, he experiences reconciliation and the promise of eternal life.

In Luke's gospel, Jesus overturns expectations at every step of his earthly journey. Where people expected a mighty political leader, they got a gentle healer and teacher. Where they expected strict adherence to the letter of the Law, they got nuance and wisdom. Where they expected earthly power, there was death on a cross. Where they expected condemnation, Jesus brought only compassion. This theme of a God who lifts up the lowly started with Mary's acclamation in the Magnificat (Lk 1:46–55) and will continue beyond the death of Jesus. The story doesn't end here, for Jesus or for us. We have Jesus' example, his words, and his risen presence with us, and he keeps surprising us. Jesus' vision is of a world with no more exclusion and where the last will be first—and that's what the Kingdom of God means. We end Year C with the powerful image of Jesus as servant King, shining like a beacon of light for the world.

> *The call to ministry is the call to be a citizen of the kingdom of God in a new way, the daring, free, accepting, compassionate way Jesus modeled. It means being bound by no yesterday, fearing no tomorrow, drawing no lines between friend and foe, the acceptable ones and the outcasts. Ministry is commitment to the dream of God.* ◆ VERNA J. DOZIER [88]

GO DEEPER

- Our journey through Luke's gospel ends here with an image of Jesus as the one who brings hope into the darkest of situations. Who in society models this Way? How are you being invited to continue the narrative?

INDEX OF SCRIPTURE REFERENCES

ENDNOTES

1   Gonzalez, Justo L., *The Story Luke Tells: Luke's Unique Witness to the Gospel*, Grand Rapids, Michigan: Wm. B. Eerdmans Publishing Co. 2015, p. 129.

2   *Gaudiem et Spes*, "Pastoral Constitution on the Church in the Modern World," Second Vatican Council, 1965, §4.

3   Pope Francis (@pontifex), "The words of the Sacred Scripture were not written to remain imprisoned on papyrus...," Twitter, 28 January 2021, https://twitter.com/Pontifex/status/1354768690949009410.

4   Keating, Thomas, *Intimacy with God*, New York: Crossroad 1994, p. 164.

5   Non-biblical second-century texts tell us that Luke was from Antioch (Turkey) and died in Greece: "Luke is a Syrian of Antioch, a physician by profession. Having been a disciple of the apostles and later having accompanied Paul until his martyrdom, he served the Lord without distraction, unmarried, childless, and he fell asleep at the age of eighty-four in Boeotia, full of the Holy Spirit."—Tenney, Silva (eds), "The Anti-Marcionite Prologues", *Zondervan Encyclopedia of the Bible Volume 5*, Nashville: Zondervan Academic 2010.

6   For an excellent reflection on the Kingdom of God see Cannato, Judy, *Fields of Compassion—How the New Cosmology Is Transforming Spiritual Life*, Notre Dame, Indiana: Sorin Books 2010, pp. 81–96.

7   Other parables found only in Luke include the parables of the Two Debtors (7:41–43), the Friend at Midnight (11:5–8), the Rich Fool (12:16–21), the Barren Fig-tree (13:6–9), the Lost Coin (15:8–10), the Dishonest Manager (16:1–9), the Rich Man and Lazarus (16:19–31), the Widow and the Unjust Judge (18:1–8), and the Pharisee and the Tax Collector (18:9–14).

8   Thunberg, Greta, "The disarming case to act right now on climate change," TEDx Stockholm, 24 November 2018.

9   Martin, James (@JamesMartinSJ), "What Jesus never said: 'Feed the hungry only if they have papers.'...", Twitter, 26 October 2018, https://twitter.com/JamesMartinSJ/status/1055848770167099392.

10 Silf, Margaret, *Wayfaring, A Gospel Journey into Life*, London: Darton, Longman & Todd 2001, p. 67.

11 Pope Francis, *Evangelii Gaudium*, "The Joy of the Gospel," 2013, §2.

12 Malone, Mary T., *The Elephant in the Church* (revised edition), Dublin: Columba Books 2019, p. 142.

13 Houselander, Caryll, *Wood of the Cradle, Wood of the Cross*, Manchester NH: Sophia Institute Press 1995.

14 Pope Francis, Homily at the Closing
    Mass for the Extraordinary Synod
    on the Family and the beatifica-
    tion of Pope Paul VI, Vatican City,
    Sunday 19 October 2014, available
    at: www.vatican.va/content/frances-
    co/en/homilies/2014/documents/
    papa-francesco_20141019_omelia-chi-
    usura-sinodo-beatificazione-paolo-vi.
    html.

15 Hays, Edward, *Prayers for a Planetary
    Pilgrim: A Personal Manual for Prayer
    and Ritual*, Notre Dame, Indiana:
    Ave Maria Press, 2008, p. 180.

16 de Chardin, Pierre Teilhard, SJ quoted
    in Harter, Michael, SJ (ed.) *Hearts
    on Fire—Praying with the Jesuits*, US:
    Loyola University Press 2005.

17 Rohr, Richard, *The Universal Christ*,
    London: SPCK 2019, p. 20.

18 Pope Francis, Homily for Holy
    Mass on the Solemnity of the
    Epiphany of the Lord, 6 January
    2018, available at: www.vatican.va/
    content/francesco/en/events/event.
    dir.html/content/vaticanevents/
    en/2018/1/6/messa-epifania.html.

19 Wallace, William, quoted in
    Geoffrey Duncan (ed.), *Shine
    on Star of Bethlehem: A Worship
    Resource for Advent, Christmas
    and Epiphany*, Norwich:
    Canterbury Press 2001, p. 234.

20 Claiborne, Shane & Compolo,
    Tony, *Red Letter Christianity:
    Living the Words of Jesus No
    Matter the Cost*, London: Hodder
    & Stoughton 2012, p. 104.

21 Bader Ginsburg, Ruth, "Rathbun
    Lecture on a Meaningful Life"
    at Stanford Memorial Church, 6
    February 2017, available at: https://
    news.stanford.edu/2017/02/06/
    supreme-court-associate-jus-
    tice-ginsburg-talks-meaningful-life,
    accessed on 15 February 2021.

22 Singleton, Tony in Radcliffe,
    Timothy (ed.), *Just One Year:
    Prayer and Worship through the
    Christian Year*, London: Darton,
    Longman and Todd 2006, p. 90.

23 Coelho, Paulo, *The Pilgrimage*,
    Harper Collins, 2008.

24 Pope Francis, Homily at Mass
    for All Saints Day in Malmo,
    Sweden, 1 November 2016, avail-
    able at: www.ncronline.org/news/
    vatican/sweden-francis-propos-
    es-six-new-beatitudes-modern-era,
    accessed on 15 February 2021.

25 This saying is commonly attribut-
    ed to Mahatma Gandhi and is very
    much in the spirit of his nonvio-
    lent philosophy. However, there
    does not seem to be any evi-
    dence that he actually said it.

26 Winn Lee, Britney "The Art of the
    Third Way," *Red Letter Christians*
    website, 17 January 2020, avail-
    able at www.redletterchristians.
    org/the-art-of-the-third-way,
    accessed on 12 February 2021.

27 González, Justo L., *The Story
    Luke Tells: Luke's Unique Witness
    to the Gospel*, Grand Rapids,
    Michigan: William B. Eerdmans
    Publishing Company 2015, p. 115.

28 Merton, Thomas in *The Asian Journal
    of Thomas Merton*, New York: New
    Directions Publishing 1975, p. 296.

29 Marilynne Robinson, *Gilead*,
    London: Hachette 2006, p. 245.

30 Tolkien, J.R.R. *The Lord of the
    Rings: The Fellowship of the
    Ring*, London: George Allen
    & Unwin Ltd 1966, p. 64.

31 Smedes, Lewis B., *Forgive and
    Forget: Healing the Hurts We Don't
    Deserve*, HarperOne, 1996.

32 Claiborne, Shane & Campolo,
    Tony, *Red Letter Christianity,
    Living the Words of Jesus No
    Matter the Cost*, London: Hodder
    & Stoughton, 2012, p. 87.

33 de Verteuil, Michel, *Lectio Divina
    with the Sunday Gospels: The
    Year of Luke, Year C*, Dublin:
    Columba Press 2004, p. 64.

34 Pope Francis, Regina Caeli, St.
    Peter's Square, Easter Monday,
    6 April 2015, available at: www.
    vatican.va/content/francesco/en/
    angelus/2015/documents/papa-fran-
    cesco_regina-coeli_20150406.html,
    accessed on 15 February 2021.

35 Hadfield, Chris (Chris Hadfield),
    "I am the astronaut Chris
    Hadfield, currently orbiting
    planet Earth," Reddit, 17 February
    2013, www.reddit.com/r/IAmA/
    comments/18pik4/i_am_astronaut_
    chris_hadfield_currently_orbiting/.

36 Silf, Margaret, *Wayfaring: A Gospel
    Journey into Life*, London: Darton,
    Longman and Todd Ltd 2001, p. 169.

37 Delio, Ilia OSF, "Internet Easter,"
    Thoughts in a Time of Crisis,
    Facebook, 6 April 2020, www.
    facebook.com/SocietySaintFrancis/
    posts/124984195803098,
    accessed on 29 April 2021.

38 Martin, James SJ, *The Jesuit
    Guide to (Almost) Everything, A
    Spirituality for Real Life*, London:
    Harper Collins 2010, p. 59.

39 Pope Francis, *Fratelli Tutti
    "On Fraternity and Social
    Friendship,"* 2020, §197.

40 Silf, Margaret, *Wayfaring, A Gospel
    Journey into Life*, London: Darton,
    Longman & Todd 2001, p. 181.

41 Perez, Iris, "God gives us Power,"
    reflection quoted in Radcliffe,
    Timothy OP with Harrison, Jean
    (ed.), *Just One Year, Prayer and
    Worship Through the Christian
    Year*, London: Darton, Longman
    & Todd 2006, p. 181.

42 Roy, Arundhati, "The Pandemic
    Is a Portal," *The Financial Times*,
    3 April 2020, available at: https://
    www.ft.com/content/10d-
    8f5e8-74eb-11ea-95fe-fcd274e920ca,
    accessed on 15 February 2021.

43 Lewis, C.S., *Mere Christianity*,
    Harper Collins, 2001, p. 175.

44 Rohr, Richard with Morrell, Mike,
    *The Divine Dance: The Trinity
    and Your Transformation*, London:
    SPCK Publishing 2016, p. 27.

45 Arrupe, Pedro SJ, "Eucharist
    and Hunger," address at the
    International Eucharistic Congress,
    Philadelphia, 1976, available at:
    https://jesuitportal.bc.edu/research/
    documents/1976_arrupeeucharist/,
    accessed on 15 February 2021.

46 Pope Francis, *Fratelli Tutti*, §287.

47 Pope Francis, *Evangelii Gaudium*, §47.

48 Prejean, Helen, "Living my Prayer," *Weekend Edition Sunday*, 6 January 2008, available at www.npr.org/templates/story/story.php?storyId=17845521, accessed on 29 April 2021.

49 Chittister, Joan, *The Audacity of Mercy*, https://www.joanchittister.org/articles/divine-mercy-audacity-mercy, accessed on 14 February 2021.

50 Chittister, Joan, *Heart of Flesh: Feminist Spirituality for Women and Men*, Grand Rapids, Michigan: Eerdmans Publishing 1998.

51 Rolheiser, Ronald, *Seeking Spirituality: Guidelines for a Christian Spirituality for the Twenty-First Century*, London: Hodder & Stoughton 1998, p. 102.

52 See Acts 9:2; 18:25; 19:23; 22:4; 24:22.

53 Solnit, Rebecca, *Wanderlust, A History of Walking*, London: Granta Publications 2014, p. 72.

54 O'Leary, Daniel, *Already Within: Divining the Hidden Spring*, Dublin: Columba 2007, p. 30.

55 McVerry, Peter, *Jesus Social Revolutionary?*, Dublin: Veritas 2008, p. 45.

56 Malone, Mary T., *The Elephant in the Church* (revised edition), Dublin: Columba Books 2019, p. 18.

57 Stewart, Columba OSB, "Prayer and Work" in *Give Us This Day*, September 2014.

58 Pope Francis, Laudato Si', §82.

59 Laurie, Hugh in Harris, Sophie, "Hugh Laurie sings the blues," *Time Out New York*, 1 September 2012, available at: www.timeout.com/newyork/music/hugh-laurie-sings-the-blues, accessed on 21 January 2021.

60 McVerry, Peter SJ, *A Dose of Reality*, Dundalk: Redemptorist Communications 2019, p. 71.

61 Pope Francis, Angelus on the Feast of the Assumption, St. Peter's Square, 15 August 2016, available at: www.vatican.va/content/francesco/en/angelus/2016/documents/papa-francesco_angelus_20160815.html, accessed on 15 February 2021.

62 Neely, Brent, "Luke 1:39–55," *A Plain Account*, 17 December 2018, available at: www.aplainaccount.org/luke-139-55/, accessed on 8 January 2021.

63 Adapted from Bourgeault, Cynthia, *The Wisdom Jesus: Transforming Heart and Mind—A New Perspective on Christ and His Message*, Boulder, Colorado: Shambhala 2008, pp. 29–31.

64 Roy, Arundhati, *War Talk*, Cambridge, Massachusetts: South End Press 2003, p. 75.

65 Pope Francis, *Laudato Si'*, §3,14.

66 Pope Francis, *Laudato Si'*, §217.

67 This gospel also occurs on the Fourth Sunday of Lent. See page 49 for another reflection on this text.

68 Greenfield, Patrick, "Humans exploiting and destroying nature on unprecedented scale—report," *The Guardian*, 10 September 2020, available at: https://www.theguardian.com/environment/2020/sep/10/humans-exploiting-and-destroying-nature-on-unprecedented-scale-report-aoe, accessed on 5 January 2021.

69 Pope Francis, *Laudato Si'*, §44.

70 Thunberg, Greta, Speech to the United Nations Climate Conference (COP24) in Katowich, Poland, December 2018.

71 "God's dream for creation is different from Pharaoh's dream or Rome's dream or Wall Street's dream. And at the centre of God's economy is the idea of redistribution....It is an invitation to holy mischief!" Claiborne, Shane & Campolo, Tony, *Red Letter Christianity, Living the Words of Jesus No Matter the Cost*, London: Hodder & Stoughton 2012, pp. 71–72. For anyone who wishes to reflect further on what "holy mischief" is about, we would highly recommend Shane Clairborne's *The Irresistible Revolution: Living as an Ordinary Radical*, Zondervan, 2016.

72 Pope Francis, *Laudato Si'*, §160–161.

73 Pope Francis, Address to participants at the meeting promoted by the Dicastery for Promoting Integral Human Development on the theme: The Energy Transition & Care of Our Common Home, Casina Pio IV, Vatican City, Friday, 14 June 2019, available at: www.vatican.va/content/francesco/en/speeches/2019/june/documents/papa-francesco_20190614_compagnie-petrolifere.html, accessed on 8 January 2021.

74 Find out more about the *Laudato Si'* Goals: www.humandevelopment.va/en/news/laudato-si-special-anniversary-year-plan.html.

75 Pope Francis, *Laudato Si'*, §85.

76 For beautiful reflections on God's presence in nature see Grogan, Brian SJ, *Finding God in a Leaf: The Mysticism of Laudato Si'*, Dublin: Messenger 2018.

77 St. Francis, "The Canticle of the Sun," available at: https://catholicclimatemovement.global/wp-content/uploads/2015/08/CanticleOfCreatures.pdf, accessed on 8 January 2021.

78 Pope Francis, *Laudato Si'*, §100.

79 Pope Francis, *Laudato Si'*, §227.

80 Beattie, Melody, *The Language of Letting Go: Daily Meditations on Codependency*, Center City, MN: Hazelden 1990.

81 Pope Francis, *Fratelli Tutti*, §64.

82 Bolz Weber, Nadia, "Sermon on "us" and "them," *Sarcastic Lutheran*, 30 September 2014, available at: www.patheos.com/blogs/nadiabolzweber/2014/09/sermon-on-us-and-them/, accessed on 15 February 2021.

83 Nouwen, Henri J. M., *The Return of the Prodigal Son*, London: Darton, Longman, Todd 1994, pp. 106–107.

84 Rohr, Richard, *The Universal Christ*, London: SPCK 2019, p. 153.

85 Dozier, Verna J., *The Dream of God: A Call to Return*, New York: Church Publishing 2006, p. 79.

86 It is worth noting that Luke is writing
    his gospel after the fall of the Temple
    in AD 70, so the events that Jesus
    describes here have already come to
    pass: the destruction of the Temple
    and Jerusalem, and the persecu-
    tion and imprisonment of the early
    Christians (as detailed in Acts). Luke
    is therefore also aware that the "end
    times" have not come, and perhaps
    his Jesus speaks accordingly.

87 de Verteuil, Michel, *Lectio Divina with
    the Sunday Gospels: The Year of Luke,
    Year C*, Dublin: Columba Press 2004,
    p. 256.

88 Dozier, Verna J., *The Dream of God:
    A Call to Return*, New York: Church
    Publishing 2006, p. 106.

ABOUT THE AUTHORS

Tríona Doherty and Jane Mellett got to know each other when they both took an undergraduate degree in theology in St. Patrick's College, Maynooth (1998–2001). They both also completed their Masters in Theology (with a specialization in Scripture) in 2003. Since 2011, they have together composed "The Deep End" reflections for *Intercom*.

Tríona Doherty is a journalist, writer, and editor. She has worked in regional journalism for more than ten years, most recently with the *Westmeath Independent*, and is a regular contributor to *Reality* magazine. Tríona has carried out editing for Redemptorist Communications, Catholicireland.net, Messenger Publications and the Carmelite Institute of Britain and Ireland. She also works with Good Shepherd Ireland to help promote their work with asylum seekers, refugees, and vulnerable women and children. Originally from Kells, Co. Meath, Tríona lives in Athlone with her husband and six-year-old son.

Jane Mellett currently works as the *Laudato Si'* officer for Trócaire. Prior to this she was a parish pastoral worker for the Archdiocese of Dublin and has worked in the area of pastoral ministry for over ten years. A native of Carlow, Jane is a qualified spiritual director, yoga teacher, and retreat facilitator. She also completed postgraduate studies in International Development in 2010 (Kimmage Development Studies Centre, Dublin). She writes for a number of publications, including the *Laudato Si'* column in *The Irish Catholic*, and has contributed articles to *Reality* and *The Messenger*.